Praise for *The Zen of Social Media Marketing*

"*The Zen of Social Media Marketing* demystifies the wacky, yet immensely powerful new world of online conversational marketing and serves as a great primer to understand where to allocate your time, money, and energy. A great read for entrepreneurs, professionals, and small businesses."

—JONATHAN FIELDS, Author of *Career Renegade*

"Building on a strong background of expert marketing advice, Shama has again produced a body of work that is at once complete and practical. This is a book that you can read quickly when you're frustrated by what seems like endless contradictions of social media, and then reference again and again as you develop your own sense of place on the social web. It is, after all, quite correctly titled *The Zen of Social Media Marketing*. I highly recommend this book."

—DAVE EVANS, Social Media Strategist,
and Author of *Social Media Marketing: An Hour a Day*

"Shama breaks down the 'why' and 'how' with easy-to-understand examples that can get you on the right track immediately...and ultimately grow your business."

—JOE PULIZZI, Coauthor of *Get Content. Get Customers*,
and Founder of Junta42

"Finally! A true authority on the subject of social media has broken through the utter noise of get-rich-quick-with-social-media hysteria. Shama takes the mystery and hype out of social media and gives readers a practical step-by-step action plan to start, grow, measure, expand, and optimize their online presence. It is a must-read for any marketing professional, C-level executive, or entrepreneur. Her conversational writing style, numerous case studies, and 'how-to' guides with screen shots make learning and implementing almost elementary. It will be *required reading* for all our clients."

—JOE ABRAHAM, Founder and Managing Director at En Corpus Group, and Author of *B.O.S.I. Entrepreneurship*

"Ready for a *true* social marketing awakening? If so, be sure and take Shama Kabani's *The Zen of Social Media Marketing* on your path to web enlightenment."

—DEAN LINDSAY, Author of *The Progress Challenge* and *Cracking the Networking CODE*

"*The Zen of Social Media Marketing* is a comprehensive guide for maximizing the marketing opportunities from online networks. Shama Kabani helps you make the most of your efforts in marketing through a stronger knowledge of social media."

—PENELOPE TRUNK, Founder of the Social Network Brazen Careerist

---

"Shama is hands-down the industry leader in social media marketing and creating buzz. She has a rare combination of social media savvy and law-of-attraction mastery that businesses clamor to find. It's easy to see why she's called the 'Shaman of social media.' She will transform your marketing and increase your sales. Listen to everything this luminary says."

—SHAWNE DUPERON, Five-Time EMMY® Award Winner, ShawneTV

"*The Zen of Social Media Marketing* is for anyone that has ever felt overwhelmed by all of the online options available now for networking, socializing, and just plain being online in general! Shama breaks it down so that even the most social media–phobes will be breathing sighs of relief at how simple she makes it all sound! Get this book today and be on your way to a stress-free online experience that you will groove and align with, thrive, and enjoy."

—SALLY SHIELDS, Author of *The DIL Rules*

4TH EDITION

The Zen of Social Media MARKETING

An Easier Way to Build Credibility, Generate Buzz, and Increase Revenue

....

Shama Hyder

BENBELLA BOOKS, INC.

DALLAS, TEXAS

BenBella

BenBella Books, Inc.
10440 N. Central Expy., #800
Dallas, TX 75231
www.benbellabooks.com
Send feedback to feedback@benbellabooks.com

Printed in the United States of America
10 9 8 7 6 5 4 3 2

Library of Congress Cataloging-in-Publication data for an earlier edition is available
upon request.
ISBN: 978-1-942952-06-0

Copyediting by Rebecca Logan and Deb Kirkby
Proofreading by Erica Lovett, Gregory Teague, Chris Gage, and Christine Koch
Cover design by Faceout Studio, Tim Green
Text design and composition by John Reinhardt Book Design
Printed by Lake Book Manufacturing

Distributed to the trade by Two Rivers Distribution, an Ingram brand
www.tworiversdistribution.com

To place orders through Two Rivers Distribution:
Tel: (800) 343-4499
Fax: (800) 351-5073
E-mail: IPSJacksonOrders@ingramcontent.com

Special discounts for bulk sales (minimum of 25 copies) are available.
Please contact Aida Herrera at aida@benbellabooks.com.

Contents

Acknowledgments

This book has been a group effort. I couldn't have done it without the entire team at The Marketing Zen Group, and special thanks goes out to Angela von Weber-Hahnsberg and David Kirkpatrick.

This book is just as much theirs as it is mine.

To our clients at The Marketing Zen Group: Thank you for allowing us to be your digital Sherpas. Thank you for your trust, your respect, and your belief in us.

And THANK YOU, DEAR READER! You have shown this book enough love to make it to a 4th edition. I hope you find this edition, too, worthy of your time and attention.

Foreword

Shama Hyder starts off her book with a scene from *The Matrix*. I know the scene well. It's a little bit of philosophy thrown into Hollywood and made simple to consume. Shama's right for giving us this gem; *The Matrix* seems to have motivated a lot of us to think differently about how we live online, and how business works.

I know. I wrote about *The Matrix* a few different times in *Trust Agents*. We could have just written, "To be a trust agent is to know how to be Neo," and it would've been a shorter book.

There is a Zen to social media. There is a way. Shama's right about that. And her way—her thoughts, her experiments, her recommendations in this book—is one that can get a lot of people closer to the prize than anything they might intuit and do on their own.

Business rules are different now. Don't believe me? How are the banks in the United States doing? How are the three big carmakers? How are small businesses doing? You want to keep marketing the way companies have been for the last fifty years? Not a good idea, I'm afraid.

We're writing new code, and Shama knows it.

There's human code out there all about how human you can be, how you can connect with people, and what that means for business. I'm flying all over the planet right now writing new versions of this code for companies, showing them how to be human. The goal is simple: explain to people that, while face-to-face is just as important as it ever was, now we've got all kinds of new tools that let us tighten bonds in between those in-person moments.

These tools leave a wake of data behind them. Follow these invisible trails of data and you can smell new customers, new opportunities. New networks don't form inside your inbox. New phone numbers don't start following you (frankly, that's probably a good thing). Social media provides the links and connections that allow these networks to form. I've taken to calling Twitter the Serendipity Engine, because that's what it harnesses: serendipity. And you, too, can harness it for your business.

Shama has a way of teaching this new code—her business-savvy Zen approach—that fits the business you're in, the person you are, and the results you want. I might do a few things differently, but we all might. (After all, if you see Buddha on the road, kill him. Isn't that the quote?) And you need to consider what parts of her approach you'll benefit most from implementing. But ignoring her isn't a good move.

Get into *The Zen of Social Media Marketing*. Keep a notepad file handy. Write down notes. Seek out everything that makes sense for you. Start setting up some next moves based on what you learn. Shama will show you.

Meanwhile, I'm waiting for the white rabbit.

—Chris Brogan,
coauthor of the *New York Times*
and *Wall Street Journal* best seller *Trust Agents*

Introduction

Why Write This?

When the first edition of *The Zen of Social Media Marketing* came out in April 2010, I was truly humbled by the amazing response we received. Readers from every walk of life and every corner of the world sent me their stories, their challenges, and their questions. Two years later, I knew the vast world of social media had changed enough to require an updated guide. Although the principles of online marketing and social media remain unchanged, new platforms, opportunities, and tools have emerged that make marketing online more efficient and easier than ever.

Social media is now an integral part of everyday life. Yet many continue to struggle with it.

A while back, I realized the *main* reason people are struggling with social media marketing: They are going against the natural order of things! The traditional marketing rules cannot be applied to social media because social media is not a marketer's platform. It belongs to consumers.

For the longest time, marketing consisted of putting out a message about a business or product that was controlled strictly by the business itself. Think about a square peg. The square peg represents the traditional marketing message. Now, imagine square holes. Each hole is a traditional marketing medium—print, radio, and television. The square peg fits the square hole perfectly.

However, here comes social media: multiple online mediums all controlled by the people participating within them—people who are busy having conversations, sharing resources, and forming their own communities. Social media is full of constant activity controlled by no one individual in particular. Unlike radio, television, and print, it isn't passive—users don't just receive content; they create it, too. Social media is a circular hole. Yet most marketers are still using a square peg. They are working *against* the grain. And they're finding themselves thoroughly stumped and no better off than they were when they started on their journey.

I wanted something I could hand to these frustrated folks, something that could help social media make *sense* to them. **I wanted something that would finally help marketers (and make no mistake—we are all marketers) understand how to utilize social media marketing concepts in a practical and efficient manner. I wanted to help them find the circular peg to fit the circular hole.**

I wanted to show them the *Zen* of social media marketing. Once you truly understand how social media functions, marketing using social media channels becomes effortless.

The Zen of What?

Yes, I know. Spending hours on social media sites only to be disappointed by a zero return on your investment doesn't put you in a Zen-like state. But that happens *only* if you are doing it wrong! If you go with the flow, you can rake in the profits *and* have fun. Imagine that!

The Zen of Social Media Marketing **is about understanding the mind-set of people who are using social media and then using it to your advantage.**

Do you remember the famous scene from *The Matrix* where Neo bends the spoon? It went like this:

SPOON BOY: Do not try and bend the spoon. That's impossible. Instead...only try to realize the truth.
NEO: What truth?
SPOON BOY: There is no spoon.
NEO: There is no spoon?

SPOON BOY: Then you'll see that it is not the spoon that bends; it is only yourself.

Social media is like that spoon. If you try to bend it, it won't bend. If, instead, you bend—if you alter your own attitude and how you market—you win. Have you ever wondered how some people rack up friends and followers, cultivate fans, and just seem to be *everywhere* at once? These people are true Zen marketers. They may not even realize they're doing anything special; they just go with the flow. They make it look effortless because so much of it *is* effortless.

Now, if you are thinking this book is just going to tell you to breathe deeply and use the force, think again. Like every good Zen master, you need some tools in your arsenal. In the following pages, I will share with you all the tools and techniques you need to become the ideal social media marketer—the guy or gal people want to be friends with and whose business gets talked about constantly.

A Personal Story

I launched my online marketing firm, The Marketing Zen Group, right out of graduate school, on my own, with no resources. Today, we have a full-time team of thirty and a global clientele. And 100 percent of our clients came to us from our online marketing efforts, specifically our social media marketing efforts. Today, we are recognized as one of the leading digital marketing companies in the world.

I continued to hire the best people to help grow our team until we became a truly full-service web agency. Whatever our clients needed online, we could provide. Soon, the business fueled its own growth. Word spread quickly; that's the nature of online marketing! I started receiving invitations to speak at top industry conferences, earned interviews with television media, and we had to start turning *away* more clients than we were taking on. As the business grew, so did my personal brand. I am humbled by and grateful for our growth.

My company is living proof that, when done right, social media marketing *works* for businesses. And it works, albeit slightly differently, for businesses of all sizes and types. I know this because we have worked with clients at all stages—from start-ups to Fortune 500s—to leverage social media. **It is my sincerest intention to share with you the same wisdom that helped our company and our clients' companies grow.** Throughout this book, you will find the stories of businesses from a variety of industries that are successfully marketing through social platforms. If they can do it, so can you!

Who Is This Guide a Perfect Fit For?

If you are responsible for marketing in any shape or form, this guide is written for you. Perhaps you are a small-business owner responsible for attracting your own customers or clientele, or the CEO of an Inc. 5000 company that wants to solidify its online reputation. Or perhaps you're a CMO looking to constantly generate inbound leads. Maybe you want to get the word out about your nonprofit. It doesn't matter; the principles are all the same. This book will show you exactly how to leverage social media to accomplish your goals.

What *does* matter is that you are

- committed to marketing or promoting your service/product/ blog/organization in an ethical and unassuming manner;
- willing to listen, communicate, and share (the building blocks of social media marketing); and
- *okay* with doing things the easy way and don't insist on going against the grain.

Social media marketing does *not* have to be a struggle.

Who Is This Guide *Not* a Good Fit For?

This guide is *not* for those who want to become overnight millionaires, internet marketers looking to turn a quick buck, or those looking to grow their Facebook friend count so they can spam those friends. Sorry to disappoint you! The strategies and techniques I lay out in this book are for legitimate businesses that will apply them with consistency and commitment—two necessary elements for social media success.

What You Will Learn

✓ Where social media marketing fits in the bigger scheme of things
✓ How to make your website or blog the hub of your online marketing efforts
✓ How to use Facebook, Twitter, and LinkedIn for online marketing in an ethical manner
✓ How to drive traffic to your sites
✓ How to navigate the constantly growing world of social media platforms
✓ How to leverage social advertising
✓ How to build credibility and establish expertise
✓ How to generate leads
✓ How to build your own community of fans
✓ How to build your e-zine/newsletter list
✓ How to measure your social media marketing efforts
✓ How to pitch bloggers and engage in Digital PR
✓ How to pitch and create strategic joint venture relationships using social media
✓ How to leverage your past success to gain future customers and clients
✓ How to get speaking engagements
✓ What you *must* have *before* you start social media marketing
✓ The #1 reason people fail at social media marketing and how to avoid that mistake

Case Studies and Profiles

In addition to the case studies peppered throughout the book, you will find a group of profiles at the end. These profiles present *real* people and businesses using social media marketing to achieve their goals. They aren't all marketers by profession but are marketing and promoting their causes successfully nonetheless.

Here's to you—a future Zen master of social media marketing! Let the journey begin.

Online Marketing Basics

BEFORE WE LOOK AT ONLINE MARKETING, let's look at traditional or offline marketing. This will help set the foundation for marketing on the internet. Before the advent of the internet, there were predominantly three main ways to market. These traditional marketing avenues were print, TV, and radio. Print included newspapers, magazines, Yellow Pages, posters, billboards, and even direct mail. Radio and TV included commercials and spots or segments. Traditional marketing worked very well for many years for three main reasons.

REASON 1: Marketing was a one-way street. Companies talked at the consumers, and this was expected because there really was no viable way for customers to talk back. Sure, word of mouth existed. However, you would realistically only tell Joe, Sally, and maybe Mary (if she was in town) before moving on. Moreover, it took a long time for word to get around. So, basically, if the nice-looking lady on television said the laundry detergent was amazing, we believed it. Today, we can go on a company's Facebook page, find them on Twitter, or even

1

comment on their blog. Customers can—and are—talking back!

REASON 2: We were all the same, more or less. Let's face it! We wore the same clothes, had the same habits, and enjoyed the same activities. It was easier for marketers to target buyers because they knew exactly who and where they were. Targeting a woman in her thirties? She was most likely a married mother of two and a stay-at-home mom. She put her family first and most likely went to church on Sundays. Try targeting a woman in her thirties today. She *may* be a stay-at-home mom to two kids and go to church on Sundays. But she may just as likely be a single woman focused on her career who enjoys hiking on the weekends. Today, you need a multipronged approach. You can't reach a demographic through one channel. You have to reach people through the channel of their choice.

REASON 3: We were less tired—and a little less jaded. At first, we believed the man on television when he said that his product could eliminate any stain. We believed it when the woman who reminded us of Grandma said the cookies tasted freshly baked. We believed it all—for a while. We were so transfixed by the well-written copy in the magazine or the flashy ad on TV. Today, we are a lot savvier. We check reviews, leave comments, and demand trial versions.

Does this mean traditional marketing is over? Not at all. It has, however, evolved. The internet has woven its way through every form of traditional marketing. When was the last time you got a piece of direct mail that didn't have a website address for you to visit? Every morning I listen to NPR (National Public Radio), and every morning the broadcasters invite me to tweet them my questions or fan their Facebook page.

What is online marketing? Online marketing is the art and science (dare I say the Zen?) of leveraging the internet to get your message across so that you can move people to take action. Whether that action is donating their time to your cause or buying your product or service, the goal of marketing has always been the same—to get people to take action. The tools just keep changing.

If online marketing is the act of leveraging the internet in general to get your message across, social media marketing is the act of leveraging specifically social media platforms (places where

The social media movement has provided the business owner powerful tools for reaching thousands of prospects and clients at the click of a mouse. However, without a strong business strategy and knowledge of online marketing, these tools are often used in vain. Success in this new media requires you to lead with a strong business mind-set.

To that end, ask yourself:

- What exactly am I trying to accomplish with social media and why?
- What are my readers' most pressing challenges, and how can I help them overcome these?
- What are the most effective delivery tools for my messages?
- How can I build enduring relationships and turn strangers into lifetime customers?

Mitch Meyerson,
author of Mastering Online Marketing and eight other books
(www.MitchMeyerson.com)

people connect and communicate) to promote a product or a service to increase sales.

First I want to share with you a simple framework for marketing online. This framework is necessary because social media marketing is not a stand-alone process or an outcome. So, before we delve into the specifics, we have to take in the big picture.

Successful online marketing can be broken down into three distinct components. I like to use the acronym ACT to describe the process.

The ACT Methodology

CONVERT

ATTRACT

Successful
Online
Marketing

TRANSFORM

A is for Attract. To attract means to get attention or stand out. Practically, this means attracting traffic to your website—your main online marketing tool.

C is for Convert. Conversion happens when you turn a stranger into a consumer or customer. And there is a difference between the two! A consumer may take in your information or even sample your product, but he or she may not always buy. That's okay! Over time, that consumer may become a customer. The more expensive a purchase is, the longer it may take. This means that you constantly have to work to convert people into consumers *and* customers.

T is for Transform. You transform when you turn past and present successes into magnetic forces of attraction.

Let's use Sue as an example. Sue sells quilts on the internet. So do hundreds of other people. How can Sue bring people to her website? If she has a Facebook page, she could create an album of her quilts. Jane, a Facebook friend of Sue's, looks at the pictures and instantly thinks of getting one for her granddaughter. She sees that Sue has placed a link to her website right below the pictures, so she clicks over to her site. Sue has successfully ATTRACTED Jane to her website.

With social media, you are the publisher! The sooner you realize you are a publisher, the more successful your business will be. Wouldn't it be great if people relied on you and your business to help them in their careers and personal lives? It's possible, but you have to start thinking differently about the way you market. Publishing valuable, relevant, and compelling information targeted to your customers and prospects is the answer. What's your expertise? How does that expertise relate to your customers' pain points? Then create the story and reach people where they are—through email, ebooks, blogs, social media, and more. Then watch the magic happen: you become the authority for that niche. You are the expert, and you may never have to actively sell again!

Joe Pulizzi,
coauthor of Get Content. Get Customers

Once Jane visits Sue's website, she takes a closer look at the quilts. She finds one that she thinks her granddaughter would just love as a holiday gift. She makes a note to herself that she will make sure to come back closer to Christmas. Now, what are the chances that Jane will actually be back? Very slim. Luckily, Sue has a newsletter sign-up box on her home page. She offers Jane some tips on quilt making in exchange for her email address. Jane gladly gives it; she is CONVERTED from a stranger to a consumer. Now, Sue can email Jane whenever she has something exciting to share—a new shipment, some more tips, or even news of a sale. Come Christmas, Jane receives an email from Sue reminding her to get her Christmas shopping done—and Jane buys. She is CONVERTED from a consumer into a customer.

Jane loves the quilt she receives from Sue! It even has a nice note. Jane's granddaughter loves the quilt just as much. In fact, she drags it around the house. It has become her favorite blankie. Jane just has to take a picture and send it to Sue. Sue takes this picture and shares it on her company blog. She TRANSFORMS the success with a customer into an attraction tool. She explains how each quilt leads to long-lasting memories and how happy it makes her to see her customers happy. Enter Don. Don has been thinking about purchasing a quilt for his own daughter but wasn't sure if she would really enjoy it. He just stumbled across Sue's blog after his wife forwarded him an article in which Sue was featured. Seeing Jane's granddaughter's smiling image with the quilt makes Don smile. He thinks, "If that little girl loves it so much, perhaps mine will, too." He also notes how much Sue seems to care about her customers. He buys a quilt instantly.

AHA! Zen Moment

In this book I'll be using the words "customer" and "client" interchangeably to refer to both, because there isn't much difference between them when it comes to using social media marketing techniques: you can ATTRACT, CONVERT, and TRANSFORM both with the same methods! 🧘

Through the ACT process, Sue ensures that she will never be short of customers. It is a simple yet effective process.

Start thinking about *all* your online marketing tactics as falling into *at least one* of these categories. Whenever you think about marketing, ask yourself this question: *Am I using this technique to Attract, Convert, or Transform?* Keep in mind that there are plenty of instances in which an online marketing tactic can perform multiple functions. We will cover these instances later.

Attract

Nowhere is social media marketing *more* successful and useful than in the "attracting" phase of online marketing. During the attraction phase, you are trying to drive traffic to your site and stand out from the masses.

We will look at the *how* of driving traffic later in the book. For now, let's focus briefly on what you *need* in order to make your product or service attractive online.

This may seem like a detour from social media marketing, but it is in fact the framework you *absolutely* must have to attract people to your product or service.

What do you need to attract prospects online? A great BOD!

- **Brand:** If your brand could be summed up in one word, what would it be? I will use my company, The Marketing Zen Group, as an example. Our clients use many words to describe us, but at the end of the day, the best phrase is "full service." We constantly aim to provide anything our clients may need relating to digital marketing and PR.
- **Outcome:** What's the outcome you help clients achieve? Not the process you use but the *final* result. Sum it up in one line: *Our company helps businesses grow by leveraging the internet.* Simple. We may create websites and conduct social media trainings and so on, but those are all part of the process. We do those things to accomplish a goal. That goal is to help our clients make more money. That goal is our outcome.
- **Differentiator:** What makes you *inherently* different from your competitors? The online marketing field is a competitive one. However, most marketing companies only offer one piece of the puzzle. They may offer graphic design, or optimize websites, or focus on simply consulting. There isn't anything wrong with this approach, but this is where our company, The Marketing Zen Group, decided to stand out. We recognized that many clients out there didn't have the time or in-house resources to handle their web marketing. Moreover, they didn't want to hire and manage

multiple companies and consultants. So, we offered to literally take over web marketing for our clients. In essence, we offered to become their online marketing department and drive inbound leads. It has been an amazing differentiator for us! So, your differentiator, in other words, is simply what makes you stand out.

I can't stress enough how important these principles—these basic building blocks—are to online marketing and social media marketing in particular. There is no lack of information and noise out there. As consumers, we are constantly inundated with data.

The branding principle "everything communicates" has only been magnified by the rise of social media.

To be effective in this space, you have to be clear about what you want to be known for—what your brand stands for. And then, you have to be vigilant about building an integrated marketing presence that supports your identity consistently. Due in part to the blurring of personal and professional identities online, you can "leak" messages that are incongruent with your brand. Frustrated offenders might say, "I didn't want *that* to communicate!" But it's not our choice; the experience of the target audience determines our identity, and *they* decide what to include as an element of our brand.

From its essence to its look and feel, business model, affiliations, and so on, it has never been more important to thoroughly plan your brand.

Samantha Hartley,
Enlightened Marketing (*www.EnlightenedMarketing.com*)

It is a continual grand bazaar. If you don't have the right elements, you can't stand out from the noise. If you don't stand out, you can't attract people to do business.

The #1 reason people fail at social media marketing is that they don't have a solid foundation. They don't have a brand, they don't understand the outcome they provide, and they have absolutely no way of differentiating themselves from the competition.

Social media is the ultimate amplifier. If you have a good product or service, it will be amplified until it is perceived as great.

If you have a shoddy product to begin with, that will also be amplified. Think about when you speak to your friends. Do you tell them that a restaurant you liked was *good* or do you say it was *amazing*? Inside each of us is a storyteller. We like to amplify. Social platforms and the internet in general allow us to do that. They are a megaphone for your message. The people who consistently do well using social media are the ones who were already doing well to begin with. The medium simply amplified their success.

Convert

So, what happens after you attract clients or customers? If they are an ideal fit, they convert. I say *if* they are an ideal fit because not everyone you attract will be. In our story earlier, Sue attracted Jane, who was an ideal fit. She was looking for quilts to buy. Let's say Sue also attracts Edgar to visit her site because he likes the pictures of the quilts on her Facebook profile. However, he doesn't have any use for a quilt; he just thinks they are pretty. He may never buy. And that's okay. You want to convert the Janes out there, not the Edgars.

As I mentioned previously, conversion can happen in one of two ways: (1) a stranger turns into a consumer, or (2) a stranger turns into a client or customer.

People become consumers when they subscribe to your blog, get on your newsletter list, or merely like your Facebook page (more on this later). They are *consuming* your information. At this point, they have converted. They are no longer strangers.

Why is this important? Even if they aren't paying for the content they're consuming, they are still being exposed to your company and your brand. There is an old marketing adage that says a person must come into contact with your brand seven times before he or she will make a purchase. Seven times!

Think about the last time you went grocery shopping at a big chain store. Chances are that there was some table setup that allowed you to sample a product—whether it was a new juice or old-fashioned jam. Studies show that when people sample, they are more likely to buy! This same "sample table" concept also works online. Offering people a sample of your work—whether through written content, pictures, or videos—can also lead them to buy from you.

Ideally, the formula works like this:

Consumption of Valuable Content + Time = Client

Time is a variable. Some people may buy right after sampling your product or service. Others may need much longer. Some of our clients received our newsletter for over a year before they decided to become clients. And not *everyone* should turn into a client. You only want those who are a perfect fit. The more qualified the buyer, the fewer the returns.

Consumers and business buyers want to make up their own minds about what they need without interference from noisy marketers. In fact, by the time they are ready to talk to you, they will be armed with information about your company, its people, and its products.

Benefit from this new buyer behavior by engaging with them as they search for answers. Deliver content that is relevant and compelling in their search for solutions. You can do this before they ever call you or walk through your front door.

You become the expert your future buyers can count on. Your content engenders a trusted relationship that makes it easy to buy from you. That's what content marketing is all about.

Newt Barrett,
coauthor of Get Content. Get Customers

How Does Social Media Marketing Fit When It Comes to Conversion?

Let's be completely honest about what social media *rarely* does— lead to instant clients. For example, if you are looking to put up your LinkedIn profile and immediately get swamped by client requests, you may be disappointed. I won't say that social media marketing doesn't ever lead directly to clients because it does happen, but this should not be your goal. If you want to gain clients quickly, there are better ways of achieving it.

What social media is great at is turning strangers into *consumers*. It's the perfect channel for allowing people to get a taste of your product or service—it's sampling made easy.

AHA! Zen Moment

Social media marketing works best as a tool for attracting traffic and attention. It doesn't work as well for converting strangers into clients. It's better suited to converting strangers into consumers (i.e., blog readers or newsletter subscribers), if simply because "free" is an easy sell. Free works! And over time, it can and will lead to business. 🧘

What's the Best Conversion Tool?

Your website! There is *no* getting around this one. You shouldn't be engaging in social media marketing if you *don't* have a website first. Every time I speak on the subject of social media marketing, someone inevitably asks me, "Can't I substitute a social media profile (say, on Facebook or LinkedIn) in lieu of a website?" The answer is *always* no.

Why should you have your own website and not depend on social media profiles?

- **You *own* your website.** You don't own your social media profiles. Your profile (and your hard-earned contact list) is owned by the social media site itself. If it goes "poof" tomorrow, then so does your online presence.
- **Social media profiles are limiting.** You can convey only so much information on your profile. Although it may (and should) intrigue someone, it isn't enough to make a sale. Remember, social media is not a selling tool! It is an attracting tool.

Transform

Once you have mastered the art of attracting and converting, you must transform your successes into attraction magnets. This brings the entire online marketing process full circle.

People, especially strangers, crave social proof. Social proof is the theory that we are more likely to do something when we see others doing it. This applies even *more* when the others in question are similar to us. We often decide what to do (including whether to buy) based on what others are doing. This isn't the only factor in our decision making, but it is a major one.

Social media is built on social proof. Because of this, social media is a great way to transform past successes into new attention for your company.

There are two parts to transforming:

1. **You have to do a good job.** If your service or product just doesn't deliver, you are out of luck. You can't transform a bad experience into an attraction tool. Let's say you sell a blender and it breaks. The customer tries to return it, but your overworked employee says you just don't take returns. Sorry. And good day! This is not an experience you want amplified. On the other hand, if you do a great job, it makes for the perfect story. One of our clients is K9Cuisine.com. They sell premium dog food online. Nothing too glamorous, but their customer service is amazing. They go above and beyond just delivering an order. If a client orders regular shipping, they upgrade it for no extra charge. If a customer says his dog didn't like a specific brand, they swap it out and help him find something that his dog will like. They're more than just a dog food seller; they become trusted dog nutrition advisors who care about your four-legged friend.

2. **You have to *use* your success to attract more success.** This goes beyond just regular testimonials. This involves telling your customers' *story*—the story of what they achieved

through your service or product. When K9Cuisine.com receives an email thanking them for helping Jack, the loved golden retriever, start eating again after a long illness, they ask the customer if they can share their story with others. The story then makes its way onto their Facebook page and into their tweets. Soon, lots of people know about how K9Cuisine.com helped Jack. Next time they think about Fido needing dog food, they will think about K9Cuisine .com. If they have a great experience, they may tell their friends. The cycle continues.

Traditional marketers didn't worry about who controlled the message. Online marketers today engage an empowered customer. For this reason I ask my clients to keep two principles in mind at all times:

1. Make it easy to buy. This involves telling the right story, exposing the real benefits, and making your shopping cart a one-click affair. It helps keep you focused when you are creating your online presence and figuring out how you will construct your marketing message.

2. Pick tactics last. This ensures that you won't get distracted by the latest shiny object fad before you have your essentials in place. Once you do, you can focus on picking the right tactics to really hear your customers.

Stephanie Diamond,
author of Web Marketing for Small Businesses

What Does Social Media Marketing Have to Do with This Step?

Everything! Whereas social media may not be ideal for converting strangers into clients, it's an excellent platform for sharing stories. Stories establish your expertise, attract fresh consumers, and even help convert faster.

The following are possible tools for transformation:

- Testimonials from customers and clients
- Case studies that showcase how a customer found a solution

to his or her problem (ideally the solution is your service or product)
- Video interviews with clients
- Audio interviews with customers
- Pictures of smiling clients with your products

AHA! Zen Moment

Social media platforms are a great way to showcase past and present success stories. By letting the customers speak for themselves, you can leverage social proof to attract more prospects. 🧘

Overview of Online Marketing Tactics and How They ACT (Attract, Convert, Transform)

The following table presents several online marketing methods and how well they accomplish each step of the ACT process. (Note: Search engine optimization [SEO] involves increasing the traffic to a website from search engines by causing the website to appear higher in a list of search results. SEO is discussed in more detail in Chapter 2.)

One-Minute Online Marketing Secret

Method	Attract?	Convert? Consumer or Customer	Transform?
Social media marketing	Yes	Yes: consumer, not customer	Yes
Website/blog/podcast	Yes	Yes: consumer and customer	Yes
Email marketing	No	Yes: consumer and customer	Yes
Giveaway on site to build email list	Yes	Yes: consumer	No
Search engine optimization (SEO)	Yes	Yes: consumer and customer	No
Video	Yes	Yes: consumer and customer	Yes

Have you ever heard of putting strategy before tactics? A strategy is an overall plan. It is the big picture: *what* needs to be accomplished and *why*. Tactics, in contrast, address the *when, where,* and *how.* Tactics are the way you implement your strategy.

Strategy should always come before tactics. However, most people doing business online go about this backwards. I call this the "shiny toy syndrome." They see the next cool networking site and join, or someone tells them they have to have a blog, so they start one only to abandon it after a month. I see people constantly chas-

The net comprises a gazillion splinters, most of which are businesses trying to claim their spot. So social media doesn't amount to a hill of beans unless what you're promoting stands out in that crowded marketplace. Differentiation is key, and that is why *nothing* can get along in the land of social media marketing without a clearly defined, unique, "hooky" offer. This is actually the most important part of branding—not the clever name or snappy tagline, as most think. In fact, when I brand folks, the brand is added last and naturally tumbles out of the "hooky" offer. My intention in branding folks is always to extract what is truly unique, quirky, interesting, and relevant about them and their businesses and then roll that into the offer and consequently the brand. What's hooky about you?

Suzanne Falter-Barns,
Get Known Now (*www.GetKnownNow.com*)

ing the next cool thing online without really knowing specifically what they want to accomplish. They may think, "I want to make money," but don't go further than that. And most importantly, because they don't know what they want to accomplish, they don't know how to measure the success of their tactics.

Are you trying to attract? Convert? Transform? Once you decide what your goal is, look at the preceding table to find a tactic that will help you achieve it. Then you'll also know how to measure your success. For example, if you *know* that the ad you are going to put on Google is meant to attract, then you will measure the number of visitors to your site to gauge how successful your investment was. You won't waste your time being frustrated that it didn't lead to more direct sales. If you were using a tactic to convert, you would check the number of people who subscribed to your newsletter. (Hint: These subscribers would be considered consumers! Remember: Consumption of Valuable Content + Time = Client.)

Now that you have a solid understanding of how social media fits into the bigger scheme of things, let's take a quick look at how to make the most of your ultimate conversion tool—your website!

Websites and Content Marketing

YOUR WEBSITE IS A WINDOW into your company. If eyes are the window to a person's soul, a website is the window to a company's soul. Okay, okay, so now you know why I am sticking to writing nonfiction. My point is your website is crucial.

Social media, blogging, search engine optimization, and email marketing are powerful ways of developing online leads for most business. However, it's your company's website where your prospect makes a buying decision and the sale actually takes place. Each webpage needs to provide prospects with a compelling reason to do business with you, including calls to action that gently direct them down the sales funnel, getting them to "buy now" or contact you. While an unprofessional website will derail the best web marketing campaign, a well-designed site is a powerful conversion tool that will continually deliver high-quality leads.

Rich Brooks,
president of flyte new media (www.flyte.biz)

The following are three reasons you *must* have a website.

REASON 1: It's expected! Can you imagine a business that doesn't have a phone number? No telephone? How 1800s! No website? How 1990s!

As social media grows and companies break new ground, even a website may not be enough. What starts out as "all the cool companies are doing it" soon turns into standard practice. I wouldn't be surprised if today's consumers get frustrated because they don't find the company they are trying to reach on Twitter. As communication channels increase, so does our level of expectation.

REASON 2: It's efficient. A website can multiply the number of people your business can influence exponentially.

Let's say you sell art supplies at a beautiful store. How many customers can you serve at one time? Two? Three? Maybe you are really good and you can serve four at a time. How many people can visit your website at once? Hundreds, thousands, maybe even hundreds of thousands. They can see your products, make purchases, and share you with friends—*simultaneously.*

Our website contains everything a prospect might want to know about us. It includes case studies, articles, bios of team members, and even videos! And all of that is available 24/7, whenever our potential clients might need it.

REASON 3: It converts! Perhaps the biggest reason to have a website is that it takes care of the "C" in our ACT blueprint. A website can convert visitors that you attract (using social media) into consumers and customers. You can attract all the people you want on Facebook, Twitter, and LinkedIn. But if they don't convert, what's the point?

Why Your Website Can't Just Be Good—
It Has to Be Great!

Your website is the online equivalent of your office—the place people go when they want to do business with you. It's not enough to have just any website. People expect that your website will match their perception of your business.

Let's say you meet a guy at a party, and he is dressed to the nines. He tells you that he helps business owners triple their income. You also hear from someone else that he is a successful business consultant. You chat with him for a few minutes, and you are impressed! This guy looks like the epitome of success. Then, he pulls out a business card (also fancy) and invites you to his office. You think, "My business could always use more help. It couldn't hurt to visit with this guy." So you go to his office.

Except his office is hard to find. You drive around for thirty minutes in circles before you locate the building, and when you finally find it, it's more like a broken-down warehouse. You park your car, double-check the locks, and slowly make your way in. The office is decrepit. It is a congested little room with papers strewn all around, and to top it off, it smells like cat litter.

Will you still do business with the guy? You might. But you may also see a major disconnect in his public persona and his actual business. If your website isn't up to par—easily findable and professional—this is the same disconnect people are likely to feel about you.

Our web is not the web of the 1990s. Remember when people actually "surfed the internet"? It was common and many times it was listed as a hobby. "I like to read, take long walks on the beach, and surf the internet." Surfing is over. It was easy back then because there were fewer websites. Today, there are trillions of websites, and people have a lot less patience for bad ones. Think about it. How long do you look at a website you are unsure about before you hit the back button? According to Canadian researchers, web users form first impressions of webpages in as little as fifty milliseconds (one-twentieth of a second). In the blink of an eye, we decide if we will keep looking or go back. This is why good enough isn't good enough anymore. You have to have a great website.

Another key consideration is ensuring your website is mobile-friendly. One reason to do so is that, if your website isn't, it will take a major search engine optimization hit, but the main reason is that more and more people are using mobile devices for everything from casual searches to serious research to making purchases.

You've probably experienced the frustration of visiting a non-mobile-friendly website on a smartphone and had to expand a page just to be able to read it, or tried to click a button designed to be clicked with a fine-point mouse rather than tapped with a relatively "fat" finger.

Optimization can be done by building separate websites for desktop and mobile visitors, but a better approach is to design your site using responsive design, or other similar background technology, which adjusts how your site is presented based on the size of the device being used. This means desktop visitors, mobile tablet visitors, and smartphone visitors will all have an optimal user experience. (This same optimization should also be done for your marketing emails.)

Website 911–EMS

To be great, your website must do three things simultaneously. It must Educate, Market, and Sell (EMS). Whenever I hear that someone's website isn't doing what it needs to, I always find it lacking in one of these three areas. And EMS is essential when it comes to conversion.

Imagine that all the visitors to your website are dots on a scale from 1 to 10. At 10, a visitor becomes a client or customer—the ultimate goal. Now, imagine a whole bunch of dots scattered on that scale. Some are at 1, some are at 5, and some are at 9.

The people at 1 are just being introduced to your brand. They just heard about you and have landed on your website for the first time. They need to be educated about how you work before they will buy. (Note: The bigger a sale, the longer the education process may need to be. You don't think too hard before spending $20 on a book, but you may need more time when you're buying a $20,000 car.)

The people at 5 already know you. They may even trust you. They just need to be nurtured for a while longer. They may need more education, or they may need more marketing—or they may just be waiting for the right time. If you are there when the time is right, the 5s are likely to buy. Let's say you sell Halloween costumes. I may not buy until Halloween comes around, unless another event comes along for which I need a costume. But when I do feel the need, it's important that you are already positioned as a solution.

The 9s may be ready to buy but just need the right incentive. Perhaps a final reminder? A last question answered? A discount? Whatever it is, your website needs to provide it to make the sale.

My goal here is to show you that everyone who visits your website will be at a different point on that imaginary scale. Your website—through Educating, Marketing, and Selling—has to move all the visitors who are an ideal fit to 10.

Let's take a look at which elements allow a website to serve as the ultimate marketing tool.

Seven Elements of a Great Website

A great website has impeccable design, structure, content, optimization, and maintenance. It also ideally includes a lead capture mechanism and social media integration.

DESIGN: Looks matter—so much so that scientists have a term for the way looks affect us: the halo effect. The halo effect occurs when we think something looks good on the surface and so we broaden the scope of that positive judgment to include characteristics other than outward appearance. If someone is good-looking, we infer that he or she must also have a good disposition. The same concept applies to websites. If a website looks good, we assume that the company behind it must also do good work. First impressions count. Especially online, where a visitor doesn't have much to go by except your website.

LEAD CAPTURE MECHANISM WITH FREE GIVEAWAY: The area on your website where visitors can input their name and email address is called a "lead capture mechanism." The majority of visitors to your website will not purchase right away. It's your job to make sure you give them options that allow you to stay in touch with them. Email marketing is a great way to stay in touch with website visitors and prospects. But when was the last time you were eager to give out your email address? Chances are, your visitors won't be either—unless you provide them with an incentive. A white paper, a recorded webinar, or a free report of some type is usually a good choice.

STRUCTURE: Ever visited a website and found yourself struggling to find a page...or even to get back to the home page? Too many choices boggle the mind. And when our mind is boggled, it is easier to say no than yes. The way you structure your website navigation is crucial. The structure must guide visitors through your website and handhold them (virtually) into taking action. And it must do this for visitors at every level—those who may be ready to buy now and those who are first-time visitors.

Don't forget about the structure of your mobile website as well. If you are using responsive design, you want to make sure you understand how that technology is presenting your site on differently sized devices and different operating systems. Your website's structure will necessarily need to be simplified for mobile, but just like the main version of the site, it must be able to guide visitors in a logical fashion.

CONTENT: Content is king. It is the heart of every good website and serves multiple purposes. The first purpose is to educate prospects and build expertise. This is why blogs are so heralded.

A well-written blog can help you stand out from the competition and educate your prospects. (I talk more about blogs later in the chapter.)

You can provide content in several forms: written (blogs and articles), audio (podcasts), and visual (video). Want to really kick it up a notch? Provide content in all three forms. This is not overkill; it's about appealing to the various learning preferences of a potential visitor. In this day and age, choices rule. Give your visitors a choice, and they are much more likely to choose you.

Good content builds trust and credibility with your network. It shows you are keeping up with the latest and greatest trends and information in your industry. It shows you care by sharing resources and tips with your visitors, and it helps you be seen as an expert in your field—the go-to person for all things. The more information you can share, the better. Again, this content should be syndicated throughout your social networks, helping make you a trusted resource.

Content becomes especially important if you are in the professional services industry or any business-to-business field in which expertise plays a key role. Content is also the lifeblood of search engines. Think about it: search engines are looking to serve their customers with good search results. They constantly have to separate the wheat from the chaff. They have to differentiate spam sites (websites set up specifically for the purpose of spamming people—think Viagra emails) from real, wholesome websites (like yours!). One of the ways they do this is by looking for content. The more fresh content you provide to search engines like Google to deliver to their customers, the more the search engines reward you.

SOCIAL MEDIA INTEGRATION: Be sure to make it easy for your visitors to connect with you on the social media networks through your website. Why? Remember, turning strangers into consumers is part of the conversion process. People like to consume information in different formats. One person may prefer to keep in touch with your company on Facebook, although someone else may prefer Twitter, and yet others prefer email marketing. That's why it's important to give website visitors multiple ways to stay in touch.

You also want to make it easy for visitors to share the information with their networks. Having a Facebook "Like" button and a Twitter button on each page of your site for visitors to share information on your website quickly with others is a great way to spread your information as well.

OPTIMIZATION: Optimization has two meanings here. One, your website has to be optimized internally. A website may look beautiful from the outside, but if the inside is poorly built, chances are it will start to show. For example, if it isn't coded correctly, it can look odd in certain browsers even though it looks fine in others. The World Wide Web Consortium has a tool that allows you to make sure your website is well coded. The tool can be found at jigsaw.w3.org/css-validator. You just put in your website address, and it will tell you what, if anything, needs to be repaired. The second type of optimization relates to search engines and making sure that search engines can "read" your website. This is called search engine optimization, and it is discussed in detail later in the book.

MAINTENANCE: The website of today in many ways is a living, breathing thing. In the past, you could create a website and sit back. Today, you can't. Passively keeping a website is almost akin to opening a store, stocking the shelves, and then doing nothing. You don't have to re-create the store every day or even every year, but you do need to tag products, move items around, change displays, and so on. Your website is the same way. Once you have the design and structure in place, you don't have to keep changing it. However, you do need to maintain it by adding content.

Blogging can be a great attracting *and* converting tool! People can find your posts attractive and subscribe to your blog, becoming instant consumers. Over time, they can be converted into customers. 🔥

A blog is an instantly and easily updatable website. A blog is the hub of your social media strategy, enabling you to grow your online presence as social media trends change and evolve.

Andy Wibbels,
author of BlogWild! A Guide for Small Business Blogging

Content Marketing

If you do any marketing industry reading, you've heard (and might be tired of) the phrase "content marketing." There's a reason content marketing has become such a marketing mantra; as I pointed out in the last section, content is king. If your website is the engine driving your marketing strategy, content is the fuel that makes that engine run—it's the core resource for your social media and email campaigns.

Content comes in many forms:

- Blog posts
- White papers
- E-books
- Photographs
- Infographics
- Videos
- Webinar replays
- Slideshows (such as webinar slidedecks)
- Animated GIFs
- Podcasts

- Customer reviews and testimonials
- And more!

Creative output of an almost limitless range of media can, and should, be part of your content marketing strategy; however, special attention should be paid to one of the most effective types of content—the blog.

The Million-Dollar Question: Do I Need a Blog?

You don't need a blog, but you do need fresh content on an ongoing basis. The best place to put this content is in a blog. Can you choose just to post this information on a webpage? Yes, but it isn't nearly as efficient because readers can't subscribe, and you can't keep up with your consumers to turn them into clients.

Blogsites

You can add a blog to an existing website, but you can also build a website around a blog. I am a huge fan of hybrid websites, or blogsites, where the entire website is built on a blogging platform. There are many blog publishing platforms out there, but the one we use most often is WordPress. It is the most robust platform, and many business websites are now using it as a content management system (CMS). A CMS allows you to manage your entire website like you would a blog. You get an admin console from which you can edit your site, allowing you to maintain your website and make regular changes without much technical knowledge. If you don't have a technical background or a webmaster who can make your updates, you should consider getting a content management system.

Now, let's say you have an excellent website in place with lots of wonderful fresh content. How do you drive traffic to it? Keep reading...

I started my blog four years ago and always had it separate from my business website. Right before my book launched this year, I decided to move to an integrated "blogsite" platform on WordPress for the following reasons:

- **Effort and resources:** It was taking too much time to update both a blog and website with relevant information. And without changing information on the website, why would people come back after an initial visit? By having an integrated site, people come back over and over to read new content.
- **SEO:** I realized that I was not being efficient by driving people to two sites. It became confusing to know which link to provide when sharing my bio, and I was diluting the SEO for both sites. Now every road leads to one site, which has increased traffic and Google ranking.
- **Client conversion:** I had many people visit my blog who loved my posts but who did not have a complete picture of what I did professionally. Many did not click the link in my "About" section to my main website to find out about my products and services. Since converting to one site, I have had a twofold increase in individual coaching clients, as well as strong sales in my live workshops and membership site.

Pamela Slim,
author of Escape from Cubicle Nation

Tips for an "Optimal" Blog

There is a strategy to blogging. Here are a few guidelines to follow when creating blog posts to get the biggest bang for your buck:

- Ideally, you should blog at least two times per week, especially when starting out.
- Each blog post should be a bare minimum of 500 words, but the longer, the better. Posts of 2000 to 5000 words are the most effective.
- Be sure to use keywords in your blog. For example, if you're a manufacturer of baked goods, you want to write posts that are relevant to baking—how to bake a cake, best desserts,

WordPress is the ultimate publishing platform because it's easy to use, it's not overly complicated, and it's infinitely flexible. Sure, it's great for blogs, and that is its forte, but it's also great for non-blog websites and even ecommerce sites. Because of plug-ins and themes (especially Headway, which includes visual blog design tools), WordPress can be extended into anything you can imagine. Creating and publishing content in WordPress really is about as easy as writing an email, only instead of clicking "Send," you click "Publish." That's such a satisfying button to click on, too, because whenever you do it, you know that hundreds or even thousands of people are going to read what you wrote.

Michael Martine,
Remarkablogger (remarkablogger.com)

and so forth. (You will learn more about keywords in the following chapter covering SEO.)

- Interlink when appropriate. When you have a keyword or phrase in your blog, link it back to the page on your site that talks about that particular product or service. For instance, if you are blogging about tips for ordering a wedding cake, link the words "wedding cake" with the page on your site that talks about wedding cakes. This is a great tip for aiding in your organic search rankings.
- Use a picture in every blog post. You'll be syndicating your blog posts into your different social networks, and when the blog posts feed into Facebook, as an example, the picture will show up. People are much more likely to read a blog post with a captivating picture than one without a picture. Don't have a relevant image of your own? You can get royalty-free images on flickr.com (just be sure to search within the box for Creative Commons for images available "for commercial use").
- If using WordPress, be sure to add tags—keywords or phrases for subjects you discussed in your blog. Again, this is a great search engine optimization tool.

Solid content is really at the heart of any good online marketing campaign, and these guidelines can help you optimize your blog content to the fullest!

"It is not the job of search engine optimization to make a pig fly. It is the job of the SEO to genetically reengineer the Web site so that it becomes an eagle."

Bruce Clay,
Bruce Clay, Inc.

Search Engine Optimization (SEO)

The Art and Science of Driving Traffic to Your Website

SEARCH ENGINE OPTIMIZATION, also known as SEO, is the process of improving the position and visibility of a website on search engines such as Google, Yahoo!, and Bing. The most important reason to get higher rankings is that you will get more targeted leads and conversions, which in turn means you will get more people knocking on your door to buy your products.

The most beautiful thing about search engine marketing is how targeted it is. Traditional marketing is like a funnel, with a wide top and a small bottom. The top is the whole audience that sees your marketing effort (say, a commercial on TV or radio, or an ad in a magazine or newspaper), and the bottom is the people who might actually be interested in your product or service—the people you actually want to reach. Search engine marketing targets the bottom of the funnel. You don't get a large general audience. You get the audience who is searching for exactly what you're selling. Google will never show a user something that is not relevant to his or her search query. Google and other major search engines will never list your website high on their results page otherwise. The key to getting high search engine ranking for the audience you want is *relevancy*. Your site must appear relevant to a specific search query.

Google, as well as other search engines, uses more than 200 factors in their search engine algorithm to rank webpages. In order for your site to appear at the top of the search engines for specific search queries, you must follow strategic step-by-step guidelines to ensure that your site is search engine–friendly and fully optimized for search engines. In this chapter, you will learn how to optimize the pages on your site to get search engines to rank your site as **the most relevant** in the search query or queries your target audience is using, which will lead more business to your website.

You might have heard the saying around SEO blogs and discussion boards that "Content is King," which is true. But optimizing that content is how to ensure your site performs better than your competitors'.

Let's begin our search engine optimization process and discover how you can dominate the Search Engine Results Page with the most competitive keywords for your company.

Keyword Research

One of the most vital steps to take in starting your search engine optimization process is to identify your target audience, and the keywords those potential customers and visitors use in search engines. If you know what your customers are searching for, you will be able to build your site and marketing campaign specifically around those customers and their inquiries.

There are many legitimate keyword tools out there, but for this example we'll use the Google Keyword Planner, which provides you with keywords users are searching for on Google.com, to identify our target audience and build our keyword research from the ground up.

To use this tool, you'll need to register for a free Googe AdWords account at https://adwords.google.com/. Once you're signed up, click on "Keyword Planner" under Tools.

It looks like this:

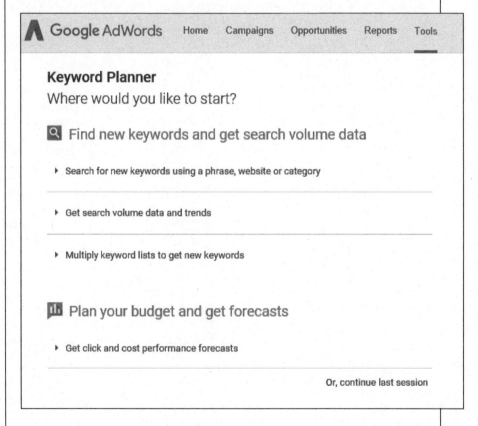

Click on "Search for new keywords using a phrase, website or category" to launch.

Let's say we're building a site for a company that specializes in fundraising. Type "Fundraising" into the "Your product or service" box and click "Get ideas."

Keyword Planner

Where would you like to start?

🔍 Find new keywords and get search volume data

▾ Search for new keywords using a phrase, website or category

Enter one or more of the following:

Your product or service

For example, flowers or used cars

Your landing page

www.example.com/page

Your product category

Enter or select a product category ▾

Targeting [?]

United States 🖉

English 🖉

Google 🖉

Negative keywords 🖉

Date range [?]

Show avg. monthly searches for: last 12 months 🖉

Customize your search [?]

Keyword filters 🖉

Keyword options 🖉
Show broadly related ideas
Hide keywords in my account
Hide keywords in my plan

Keywords to include 🖉

Get ideas

Once your results load, click on the "Keyword Ideas" tab to display the list of relevant keywords.

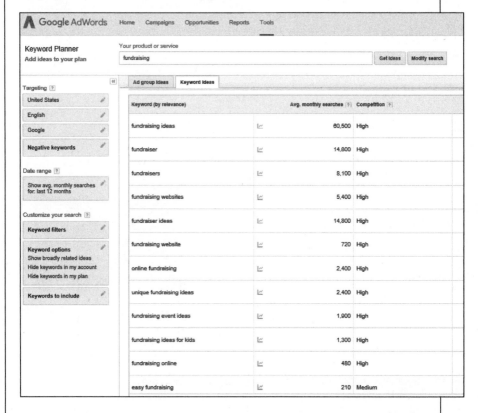

Begin your keyword research by searching for broad keywords. As you continue, drill down to more specific keywords within your industry. This will help you reach a more specific target audience. For example, type in "raise money for" under "Keywords to include" on the left.

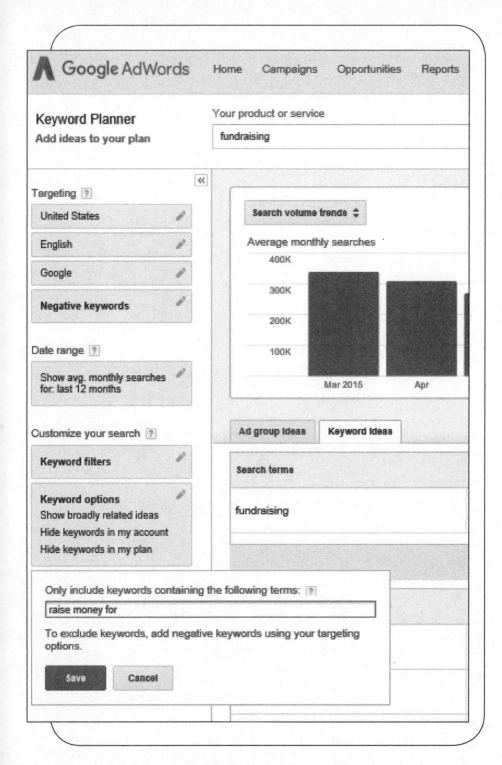

You will get the following results:

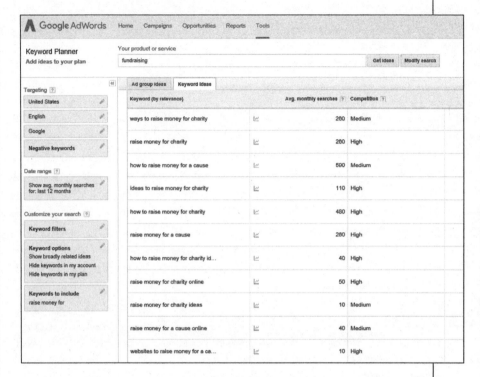

Notice that there are quite a few searches for keywords such as "how to raise money for a cause," "ways to raise money for charity," and "how to raise money for charity." These are all great keywords that you can use to expand your site's content and pages.

Google allows you to download each list of keywords you generate with your searches to a separate file. This is a great process to help you stay organized. When you finish a keyword search session, click on "Download."

Download historical statistics
Keywords: 32

Segmentation	☐ Segment statistics by month
File format	○ AdWords Editor CSV
	You'll be able to import this format into AdWords as a spreadsheet. Learn more
	◉ Excel CSV
Destination	☐ Save to Google Drive

Download Cancel

Then export the list as an "Excel CSV" file.

Organize your Excel file by grouping your keywords into categories. Every category will contain a set of keywords associated with it. For example:

	A	B	C
1	Category	Keyword	Global Monthly Searches
2	Fundraising	fundraising	1000000
3	Fundraising	fundraising ideas	165000
4	Fundraising	school fundraising ideas	12100
5	Fundraiser	fundraiser	450000
6	Fundraiser	fundraiser ideas	201000
7	Fundraiser	school fundraiser ideas	14800

The Fundraising category will have keywords such as fundraising, fundraising ideas, and school fundraising ideas. The Fundraiser category will contain the keywords associated with it: fundraiser, fundraiser ideas, school fundraiser ideas, and similar phrases.

Note: You should export all the CSVs and then combine them into one document yourself. This will ensure that you have all your keywords in one spot.

This keyword identification process will assist you throughout the duration of your search engine marketing campaign, as you create new content or edit your existing content to include these keywords.

More Keyword Research

Keyword research is an ongoing process. You can always find and identify other keywords potential customers are searching for as your business grows and develops. In particular, there are two easy-to-use tools that can help you keep your keyword list up-to-date.

Google's keyword suggestion function is a great way to identify additional keywords you may have missed. In the following example, we are trying to find additional keywords Google suggests to its users (which are based on what others are currently searching for) when typing "how to raise money" into the search box:

how to raise money for charity
how to raise money **for charity**
how to raise money **fast**
how to raise money **for a cause**
how to raise money **fast for kids**

Google suggests that the phrases "how to raise money fast" and "how to raise money for a cause" would be very useful keywords to use in optimizing specific pages on your site tailored to different audiences.

Google's "Searches related to" feature is another tool to identify additional keywords. Go to Google.com and type in "Fundraising ideas." Scroll down the page to the very bottom, and you will see:

These keywords are more useful additions to your list and can help you with further keyword research using Google's keyword suggestion function. Hang on to this keyword list, because it provides you with greater insight into the minds of your consumers. You can also use your keywords for topic ideas when working on blog posts or content for your website.

Technical Issues with Your Site

Site architecture is your approach to the design and planning of your site. Google, as well as other major search engines like Yahoo! and Bing, pay close attention to how your site is built in order to determine if the site is "good enough" to be listed at the top of the search engine's pages. Everything from your site's navigation menu to hidden files and broken links and more can affect your site's rankings. If your website is not coded correctly, your site's architecture can actually get your website ranked behind your competitors'. It's very important to check certain elements in order to ensure your site is search engine–friendly and ready to be easily "crawled" (reviewed for results page inclusion) by the search engines.

- **Google Webmaster Central:** This tool ensures that your site is search engine–friendly. It will identify various issues, such as broken links, malware, crawling issues, and other problems, as well as providing data on search engine indexing and search traffic. If you sign up for this tool, Google will also send you messages if it finds issues with your current site. To create an account, visit www.google.com/webmasters.
- **Sitemap.xml:** A sitemap is a file that lists all the pages that you want the search engines to crawl; it's like a glossary for

Google. Generate a sitemap.xml and upload it to the root directory of your server. Then submit it to Google Webmaster Central.

- **Site speed:** Ensure that your site loads quickly. There are many free tools that can be found online to test loading time. Use them to compare your site to the top sites on the first page of Google. If your site loads slower than your competitors', ask your website developer or programmer to take steps to improve your speed: clean the code your site was written in, reference java script codes, and reduce the size of large images, just to name a few examples. You can also have your programmer check various advanced server issues. However, sharing a server with other websites or webhosts can sometimes cause problems that you might not necessarily be aware of but which slow down your site.

- **Google Analytics:** This tool tracks how visitors are getting to your site and generates advanced traffic reports. To create an account, visit http://www.google.com/analytics.

- **404 page error:** A 404 page is a custom error page that appears whenever a visitor accidentally arrives on a page of your site that no longer exists or, in some cases, never existed. For example, let's say a visitor was trying to get to your services page, and misspelled the exact URL. A 404 page should come up to help them. This makes for a better user experience, which search engines value. Also, search engines like knowing which pages exist and which don't. Your 404 page should be customized to contain a message to the user telling him or her that the page was not found, plus a call to action to continue browsing your site, such as alternative pages to visit.

- **301 Redirect:** Google treats http://Domain-Name.com and http://www.Domain-Name.com as two different sites. This means your website's SEO is penalized. To avoid this, create a 301 redirect from Domain-Name.com to www.Domain-Name.com. If you currently have an .htaccess file on the root, simply add the following code to it:

```
RewriteEngine On
RewriteCond %{HTTP_HOST} ^Domain-Name.com [NC]
RewriteRule ^(.*)$ http://www.Domain-Name.com/$1 [L,R=301]
```

(Just make sure your website does in fact redirect to the www
.Domain-Name.com after updating the .htaccess page.)

- **301 Permanent Redirect**: If you are redeveloping a website, your pages may end up with new URLs. A 301 permanent redirect ensures the search engines know that your old pages have moved to a new location. If you don't do this, your site may lose the SEO value that your old pages acquired over the years.
- **Robots.txt**: Your site may include data you do not want to be searchable. To ensure that search engines do not crawl and index sensitive information, use a robots.txt file, which tells search engines not to crawl specific areas of your website. You can add the robots.txt file to the Google Webmaster tool.
- **Broken Links**: Search engines don't like when sites link to pages that have been deleted or moved. Ensure that there are no links like this on your site by checking Google Webmaster Central.
- **URL naming**: Use your keywords to create pages dedicated to their target audience. Taking our example for the Fundraising site, you will need to name and create pages using these keywords. For example, if we have a page about fundraising ideas for schools, name your page school-fundraising -ideas.html. Remember that search engines are looking for keywords, content, and relevancy to any given unique search query.
- **Image naming**: Naming images is basically the same as URL naming. You want to name your images using the same technique. For example, if you have a page about fundraising for schools, create an image with a fun illustration of kids in school and name your file fundraiser-ideas-for-school.jpg.

On-Page Factors

On-page SEO factors are a crucial part to your site's overall SEO success; they are still an integral part of the algorithm Google and other search engines use to rank your page. On-page elements refer to the HTML tags within a site's coding—HTML is a coding language used to write webpages—and they can be tweaked to make your website more appealing to search engines.

Though other elements like sitemaps and redirects are important, it's best to concentrate on some of the major on-page factors in order to ensure that your webpages are optimized and can rank higher with search engines.

Title: The <title> tag defines the title of the page or document online—the way search engines reference your page on their search engine result pages. It's also a great opportunity to provide search engines with information about the page you are trying to optimize.

For example, go to Google.com and type in the following keywords: *fundraising ideas.* You will see the following results:

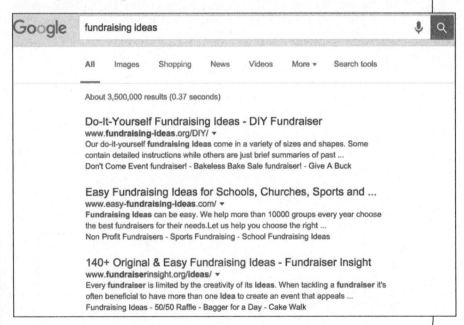

Here's the Title tag of the first result:

<title>Do-It-Yourself Fundraising Ideas – DIY Fundraiser </title>

As you can see, the title contains its site's most relevant and important keywords: *Fundraising Ideas* and *DIY Fundraiser*. These sites are optimized for the search phrase "Fundraising ideas" because the keywords appear in the title, among other factors.

Each page of your site should have a unique title that uses three to five keyword phrases and is less than sixty-five characters long. Any characters following the sixtieth one will be ignored. You should avoid "stop words" between important keywords such as *and, or, with, for.* You have limited space to write a title and you want to use as many of your main keywords as possible. Dashes are one good way to separate keywords, but do not overuse them. This can be viewed as keyword stuffing (a big no-no) by the search engines. You can use commas, pipe bars, and sentences that make sense to humans, too.

Meta description: The description tag describes, in a couple of sentences, what a page is about. For example:

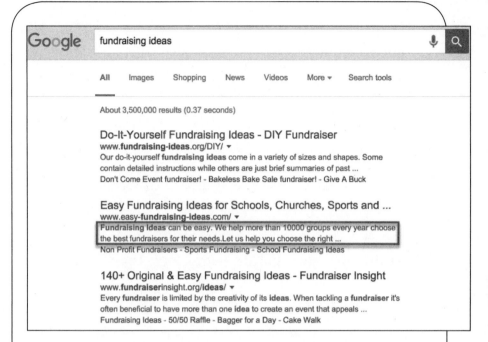

The HTML code that generated that second result:

> <meta name="description" content="Fundraising Ideas can be easy. We help more than 10,000 groups every year choose the best fundraisers for their needs. Let us help you choose the right fundraiser." />

When writing a meta description, ensure it is no more than 150 characters in length. Write a unique meta description for each page and the main keywords you are optimizing your page for.

Headings: Search engines use heading tags to tell them of the relative importance of text on a webpage. Your webpage readings should include the most relevant keyword phrases and be wrapped in heading tags, like this:

> <h1>Most relevant keywords</h1>
> <h2>Second most relevant keyword phrases</h2>
> <h3>Third most relevant keyword phrases</h3>

The best way to optimize the headings on your page is by assigning a heading tag for various relevant paragraphs within your content. The most important tag is the <h1> and is used at the top of the page.

<h1>Fundraising Ideas</h1>

The rest of the heading tags can be used for specific short phrases describing the previous tag and the content associated. For example:

<h2>Easy Fundraising Ideas</h2>

Follow up with a <h3> heading further down the page that drills down further, such as:

<h3>How Do I Start My Own Fundraiser?</h3>

Keep in mind that your headings must always describe the paragraph or paragraphs that follow it.

Bold, italic, underline, bullet points: Search engines also pay attention to the tags for bold <b>, italic <i>, underline <u>, and bullet points. Use these features to highlight search terms, but be sure to do so tastefully.

Internal linking: One of the best-kept secrets to advanced optimization is internal linking between pages. Internal linking between pages helps Google as well as other search engines understand the relevancy of keywords or keyword phrases to your page content by using what's called "anchor text"—the text that visitors click on to go to another page. For example, let's say you have a page that talks about *fundraising for elementary schools*. This text can be linked to another relevant page on your website that describes *fundraising ideas for kids in school* like this:

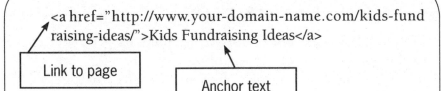

```
<a href="http://www.your-domain-name.com/kids-fund
raising-ideas/">Kids Fundraising Ideas</a>
```

Link to page

Anchor text

This is a great way to connect relevant content within a website and target additional keyword phrases.

You may want to use descriptive phrases to link between pages. For example: *the easiest way to raise money for school* would be a great anchor text link to a page that talks about raising money for schools.

Internal linking is also a great way to introduce pages deep within your site (that is, pages that would otherwise take four or more clicks to reach from the home page), so that search engines can crawl and index them.

Image ALT tag: Sometimes, search engines are specifically looking for images, so optimizing your images for these searches can help you reach new customers via image channels like Google Images and Bing Images. The best way to optimize an image is by describing the picture in a few words (focusing on your main keywords, of course). For example, let's say we have an image showing Boy Scouts collecting money for their fundraiser. This would be a good picture to optimize for "boy scouts fundraising ideas." The HTML code will look like this:

```
<img src="boy-scouts-fundraiser.jpg" alt="boy scouts fund-
raising ideas" />
```

On-page factors are a great way to tell the search engines what your site is about but stay true to your target audience; optimize your pages with the most relevant keywords related to the content of the page. Do not optimize your page for apples when you're talking about oranges.

Link Building

Link building—the process of getting links back to your site placed on other sites in order to increase your site's rank with search engines—is one of the most misunderstood areas of Search Engine Optimization. Let's start by defining what "backlinks" are.

Backlinks are links that point to a website. Let's say a webpage includes the text "RecipesABC has the best chocolate cake recipes in the world" and the words "chocolate cake recipes" link back to www.RecipesABC.com (not an actual site).

What does that mean to search engines?

By providing a link back to RecipesABC.com with the anchor text "chocolate cake recipes," we are telling search engines that RecipesABC.com is relevant to "chocolate cake recipes." The search engines register this as a vote for RecipesABC.com's web popularity, which affects its rank among other relevant sites with the same anchor text "chocolate cake recipes." The more votes to your site, the better rankings your website will achieve when users search "chocolate cake recipes."

Here are a few important factors to remember about link building:

Relevancy: Always seek backlinks from relevant websites. If you have a website that sells a dessert recipe book, make sure to seek links from websites that are relevant to your topic, i.e., other recipe websites, book stores, chef's blogs, home cooking, bakeries nearby, and so on. Their "votes" will mean more to search engines on the subjects you're targeting.

You can use www.dmoz.org to find more topics relevant to the theme of your site.

Website authority: One of the most important things to remember about link building is that not all links are created equal. In the eyes of search engines, a link pointing to your website from the *New York Times* is a lot more authoritative than a link from a website that was created yesterday.

You can use http://who.is to discover who owns a website and when it was created, among other relevant details.

Note: Beware of link farms! A link farm is a website set up with the sole purpose of increasing incoming links for other websites. These sites are usually made up of long lists of unrelated links and are considered a form of spam.

User experience: Google, as well as other search engines, are looking for websites that provide the best user experience. If users can't find what they are looking for, search engines will consider the site less trustworthy. If you see a site that is not so user-friendly, skip your link-building efforts there and focus instead on sites that provide a friendlier user experience.

There are many ways to build links back to your site. Here are a few ideas:

- Reach out to relevant blog owners and pitch an interesting story.
- Share your website content on Twitter, Facebook, and Google+, and via quality social bookmarking sites like Digg, Reddit, and StumbleUpon.
- Add sharing options on your website to make it easier for other people to share your stories via social bookmarking sites, social media sites, and email.
- Participate in group discussions and forums related to your industry.
- Participate in Q&A sites, like Yahoo Answers, WikiAnswers, and Quora.
- Contribute to relevant blogs by posting comments on their stories.
- Connect with others whose sites share the same theme or niche as your website and offer them a reason to link back to you.
- Run a promotion or contest on your website. Design a badge and provide the HTML code so your visitors can link back to your website simply by copying and pasting a badge.

- Submit your website to relevant quality directories. Some helpful search terms to consider when looking for relevant directories include:

  {keywords} + "add url"
  {keywords} + "submit url"
  {keywords} + "directory"

- Write press releases about your company and submit them to PRWeb.com and other PR sites.
- Write unique articles related to your industry and distribute them to e-zine articles sites, as well as to social media platforms such as squidoo.com and blogger.com.
- Submit your business information to relevant sites like Google Places, Bing Business Portal, Facebook Places, Yelp, Insider Pages, Yellow Pages, and others.

Remember, when asking others to link to you, always request that the link use specific anchor text keywords. This will get your website higher on the search engine results pages for the specific keywords you've been targeting.

Also, always stay relevant by posting only insightful articles and comments on other websites, not spam.

SEO, simplified, consists of this: (1) a well-built website, (2) lots of relevant and timely content, and (3) links back from other credible websites. Don't let the technical aspects overwhelm you too much. Of all web marketing activities, SEO is the most outsourced of them all; the goal for this chapter was just to give you an educated overview. Now, let's move on to social media!

4

Social Media Marketing
What You Need to Know Before You Start

The Nature of the Fun-Loving Beast

Now that you have a solid understanding of online marketing, we can move on to social media marketing. Let's break down the phrase "social media marketing."

- **Marketing**: Promoting a product or a service to increase sales
- **Social media**: Online platforms where people connect and communicate

Some examples of online platforms are blogs; social networking sites such as Facebook, Twitter, LinkedIn, and Instagram; and video sites such as YouTube.

Most marketers abuse social media platforms. They use them to push their message on people and try to dominate the market. Remember our discussion about the mistake of going against the

What Social Media Is All About

I chose to explore the social web as a business framework after reading Tim Berners-Lee's talk honoring Vannevar Bush at MIT in 1995, excerpted in part here:

I [have] a dream that the web could be less of a television channel and more of an interactive sea of shared knowledge [and that] by working on this knowledge together we can come to better understandings.

This crystallized for me what social media is all about, conveying the importance of participating with rather than attempting to impress upon your customers. The social web is a place where people gather and share to improve their condition. As marketers, it is our obligation to respect this fundamental premise. It is our gain when we do and our loss when we don't.

Dave Evans,
author of Social Media Marketing: An Hour a Day

grain? This is a great example. Marketers who abuse social media usually do so because they are used to using traditional marketing methods like television. You can't talk back to the TV. (Well, you can, but it doesn't get you very far.) With social media, talking back is the whole point; it's a conversation, not a monologue.

Chapter 1 discusses how traditional marketing has evolved over the years. Now let's take a look at a table of descriptive words and phrases that compares traditional marketing and online marketing—specifically, social media marketing.

Traditional Marketing	Online Marketing/Social Media Marketing
Dominate the market	Create a community within the market
Shout out loud	Listen, and then whisper
Me, me, me	Us, us, us
Push the product or service	Pull in people with your message/story
Advertising	Word of mouth
Control	Allow
Pursue "leads"	Nurture relationships

Why Social Media Marketing? Why Bother?

According to multiple surveys and studies, between 49 and 90 percent of web users have made a purchase based on recommendations they received through a social media site—an impressive percentage even at the low end. Roughly 40 percent of small businesses have a Facebook page, and many fewer use other social media platforms (a little over 10 percent use Twitter). Marketers are missing out on a huge opportunity to connect with potential customers. Social media marketing is a good idea for the following three reasons.

1. **Social media sites are where the *people* are.** Let's say there was an expo happening with *1.55 billion attendees,* and I offered you a free booth. Would you take it? I sure hope you would. That's how many people are using Facebook. If Facebook were a country, it would be the most populous nation on Earth. And it costs nothing to join.

2. **Trust in advertising continues to erode.** Let's face it. We trust our friends more than we trust what the nice folks on TV tell us. You can either *be* that friend or you can be the voice on TV that gets ignored. The call is yours. But you can't fake it. Because of the transparent nature of social media, you can't really hide who you are for long. Let's say a company pretends that they value their customers more than anything. Then they turn around and treat a customer badly. That customer has a voice. Chances are she has a Facebook profile or Twitter account. Even if she doesn't, she may tell a friend who does.

3. **People are already talking about you.** That last example tells us something else, too: people are already talking about your products, your service, and your company. It's inevitable. Social communities are breeding grounds for interaction. The only choice you have is whether you join the conversation. Every individual who interacts with your company has the potential to become a champion or a critic. You get to determine which one they become.

Two of the most powerful benefits of social media for small business are access and prominence. Tap your blog to demonstrate thought leadership (aka prominence) in your niche, and then leverage Twitter and Facebook to expand the conversation, facilitate evangelism, and grow your "following." As an example, Twitter lets you find highly relevant conversations with prospective clients, vendors, mentors, and colleagues in real time; join in, demonstrate value, and then, if appropriate, offer solutions to any problems being discussed. Do this on a regular basis and you'll grow a sizable tribe primed for your products and services.

Jonathan Fields,
author of Career Renegade

Social Media Marketing Tenets

Before we delve into the nitty-gritty of specific social media platforms and how to make the most of them, let's look at the tenets of social media marketing. These principles do not change, regardless of the technology in question.

- **Respect other people online.** Whether you're using email or instant messaging (IM) or social media: (1) don't spam people, (2) don't blindly add people to your email list, and (3) respect people's "virtual space." Basically, follow the Golden Rule; if it would annoy you, it will doubly annoy another. The same common rules of etiquette that apply offline apply online, too. Would you ever run up to someone, hand him your business card, and run away? I hope not. Yet people often do the online equivalent: post their website link—their virtual business card—blindly on people's online spaces.
- **Efforts to control or manipulate will backfire.** Did you hear the story of how the CEO of a top grocery chain got busted for pretending to be a customer and praising the company in forums? It was quite a scandal. Once his identity was

made public, it was all over. It's next to impossible to manipulate people online without getting caught. And because there are *so many* better ways to go about influencing people positively, there is no need to control the conversation.

- **Don't chase everything new under the sun.** This is a common mistake many people make when first starting out. Remember "shiny toy syndrome"? Resist the temptation to grab at everything. Do your research, pick one or two methods, and work at them consistently. This is the reason I am not covering every social media channel that's out there in this book. I've chosen instead to focus on the ones that I believe provide the highest return on investment.

- **Traffic is nice but should not be the only goal of social media marketing.** Some people out there look at social media marketing *only* as a means of attracting traffic to their websites. Although traffic is a great goal and easily measurable (it falls under Attract), it should not be your only goal. Remember, you can and should use social media to transform as well. It is a great way to share your stories, listen to feedback, and cultivate relationships with potential customers and future partners and vendors.

- **It's a good idea to use your real name.** Nine out of ten times, it's best to use your real name—even if you represent a company. Why? People don't want to be friends with McDonald's or Dell. They want to connect with others like them. We cover later when it is advisable to use your business name.

- **You have to be proactive.** This is not the same as being pushy. I hear the following a lot: "I am on Facebook and LinkedIn, but it doesn't seem to do much." My response is usually: "What exactly did you expect 'it' to do?" It's like saying you went to a networking event that didn't do anything for you. The real question here is what did *you* do at the networking event? Did you reach out to two people and have a conversation? Social media is only what you make of it.

Social Media Marketing Checklist

The following is a list of what you *must* have in place (or be in the process of putting in place) before you start with social media marketing. Remember—social media marketing is only part of the bigger picture.

- ✓ **A good BOD**: You must have a keen understanding of your brand, outcome, and differentiator.
- ✓ **A website**: Remember EMS. Your website must educate, market, and sell!
- ✓ **Content**: Ideally, your website will include a blog, because a blog makes it easy to update your site regularly with fresh content, but however you update, just make sure you do. Fresh content increases the likelihood visitors will stick around and turn into consumers.
- ✓ **An email capture mechanism**: Don't send people to your website unless you have a way to follow up with them. Ideally, this means collecting their email addresses so you can send them relevant content in the form of a newsletter or bulletin in the future.

Have all four? You're ready to rock and roll!

Visibility + Credibility = Real Social Media Success

By using social media to position yourself as an expert in your field, you'll stand out from competitors, generate buzz, and increase your value. To do this, you must market yourself as a highly visible, ideally matched source of information for your audience.

Always focus on providing valuable content, boosting your credibility, and building trust. When done correctly, you'll turn followers into loyal fans who practically do your marketing for you.

Value, credibility, and trust. Add those three things to a high level of visibility and you have the social media recipe for success.

Nancy Marmolejo,
Viva Visibility (www.VivaVisibilityBlog.com)

Which Technologies and Networks Do I Use?

Although there are thousands of social networking sites and technologies out there, in this book, I will be focusing only on the "big three" (though a later chapter addresses other valuable platforms, including Instagram, which may soon join the big three, and Pinterest, a platform for marketers looking to reach a female demographic):

- Facebook (www.facebook.com)
- Twitter (www.twitter.com)
- LinkedIn (www.linkedin.com)

I also cover certain technologies that complement social media marketing, including online video.

There's really only one way "social" and "marketing" can coexist happily. And that's if you take off your marketing hat when thinking about social media marketing and, instead, think like an average user of social media.

Allow yourself to become engrossed in the user experience on social media sites. Watch for things like how the particular "culture" of each site is constructed and maintained. Watch for things people say and do that would lead nicely into relationship building, which leads to new clients, branding, or product sales.

Since it is impossible to completely forget that you are a marketer, you will still pick up on great ways to increase business through social media, but you must think like a user first and a marketer second.

Social media users are there for anything but advertisements and pushy marketing. But make no mistake about the fact that marketing is being done successfully on these sites. It's called social marketing for a reason, and it's a very different thing that you can only see when you have your user goggles on.

Once you understand the main purpose of any social site, you can do a lot to increase your traffic and grow your business with social media in ways that don't turn off users but that engage, intrigue, and excite them.

Jack Humphrey,
FridayTrafficReport.com

For each of the three networking sites, I'll tell you:

1. Why to bother with it
2. How to use it
3. Do's and don'ts
4. Specific marketing tactics

Ready? Let's get started!

> "Giving is better than receiving because giving starts the receiving process."
>
> Jim Rohn

Identity Before Community
Why Most Companies Fail at Social Media Marketing

WHEN I WAS DOING my graduate studies in 2008 at the University of Texas at Austin, I was enamored by the world of social networking. This was a time when Twitter had just a few thousand users, and only the über-geeky were making it their playground. I was fascinated by how people pontificated on world-changing ideas in one breath (err...tweet) and shared the mundane (eating a PBJ!) in the next. I was hounded by one simple question: What compelled people to use social networking in the first place?

I theorized (as good academics are taught to do) that people craved community. They wanted to connect with each other and create communities around this very human need for connection. I was wrong. My research led me to believe that this was only a secondary reason for most social media users. The fundamental reason was that social networking sites allowed people to showcase their own identity.

Take a second to let that fully sink in. Go back and reread that sentence, if you like. People weren't clamoring to stay connected; they wanted to, first and foremost, see their own identities reflected on the web. If most businesses and organizations looking to make a dent online truly understood this, it would change how they go about their campaigns entirely. They'd aim to put their audience's brand first rather than just push their own company brand.

I did an interview with Jeff Haden of *Inc Magazine*[1] on this very topic, and the feedback was so tremendous that I've included it here to further shine a light on this concept.

Here is some of that interview:

Jeff: You realize this premise [that identity trumps connection on social networks] is completely opposite from what most people think? Social media is supposed to be about connection, not reflection. (Sorry, couldn't resist.)

Shama: And that's why most businesses get poor results. A social site is as much a digital mirror as it is a social platform. Connection starts with understanding the meaning and impact of that reflection.

Jeff: You're going to have to explain that.

Shama: I did my graduate thesis on Twitter back when it only had only a few thousand users. My first questions were, "Why would people tweet? Why would they share what they are doing?"

While I was doing the research I had this lightbulb moment. My original hypothesis was that we use social media to connect with one another, but I found the primary reason we use social media is to showcase our own identities.

Jeff: So we're all a bunch of narcissists.

Shama: It's not narcissistic at all. It's like in kindergarten (in a good way): You're having a peanut butter and jelly sandwich, and the kid next to you says he likes peanut butter and jelly,

---

[1] http://www.inc.com/jeff-haden/basic-social-media-marketing-mistake-everyone-makes.html

and then he says he likes blue crayons, and you like blue cray-ons…That's how we make friends and become who we are. We showcase our identities, and based on the reflection or reaction of other people, we tweak our identities.

The same is true when you're a teenager and, say, your friends like rock music. They wear certain clothes…so you do, too.

The only difference is that now all that is online. Think about Facebook profiles; Facebook really gets the idea that people, first and foremost, want to showcase who they are. Social media is like a mirror we hold up to show how we are unique and special.

It's like we're decorating the inside of our lockers again. We just transferred that to the web.

The platforms have changed, but have the principles of how we behave and how we express ourselves? Not really.

Jeff: I get that. A friend loves to add stuff to his Facebook time-line. I tease him because he acts like a painter finishing a mas-terpiece. When he's done, he's a little too pleased with himself. (I know you said it's not narcissistic, but in his case I'm not so sure.)

But I'm not sure how understanding that helps a business improve its social media marketing efforts.

Shama: Here's how. Most companies still focus on the secondary aspect: getting *them* to connect with *us*. Too many companies say, "Business is about marketing and branding. We will create a brand. We will tell people who we are."

That's backward. Realizing that social media is a mirror forces companies to think not about what they want their brand to be, but what their brand says about the individual.

And that's why a cupcake shop can rack up more "likes" than a major corporation. Liking the little cupcake shop down the street says something about me as an individual: Maybe they only use organic ingredients and that's important to me. Or maybe they donate a portion of their revenue to a charity I support. In some way, that cupcake shop is a reflection of my identity and an extension of my identity brand. It reflects something I see in myself.

Liking a big company...what does that do for me? Not much. What does that say about me? Nothing.

Jeff: That's probably why I've never felt compelled to "like" a big company. (Maybe that's why I don't even have a Facebook account.)

Plus, there's the association factor. If I like a fast-food chain, I'm not going to declare it publicly. I'm not going to like an athlete's foot powder or a dandruff shampoo or adult diapers. (Not that I need any of those!) That would not only say something about me; it would say too much about me.

But I would like my local bike shop because they lead local bicycle advocacy efforts, help build new trails...and they're great guys. So liking them would say something I would feel good about saying.

Shama: For a business, what matters most is not what your brand says about you—it's what your brand says about the people you want to interact with.

The heart of building a community, whether you're a B2B or a B2C, is recognizing what that community cares about. It's not manipulative; it's not sneaky—it's the most authentic way to brand your business and grow a following online.

It's not manipulative because it's about what you do, not what you say. It's about what you do and what that says about the people who like you for doing it.

Jeff: I see and hear stuff like "Like us on Facebook!" or "Follow us on Twitter!" all over the place, and I always wonder what the business is thinking. Why would I? You haven't given me a reason.

And I'm immediately turned off when I have to "like" a business to get a discount or special offer. But maybe that's just me.

I wouldn't feel a connection to the company. It would just be a transaction. "Here's my like, now give me my discount."

Shama: There's a much better approach that doesn't require incentives or promotions. (Although there is nothing wrong with either.)

I was speaking at a real estate conference and a number of people said they were frustrated because they had created social media platforms for their real estate businesses and nothing was happening. The problem was they had sites . . . but those sites didn't say anything about the people they wanted to engage.

But if they changed their focus and created a site like, say, "Why Dallas Rocks," and it was powered by Dallas Realtors . . . then you can get "likes" because it says a lot about me: I like my city, I like my community . . . and I like you for getting that.

The same is true for a wedding site. Say you sell bridal gowns—how many people are going to follow you? Change the focus. Create a site like "All About Brides," or "I Can't Believe I'm Engaged," or "OMG I'm Engaged!" . . . powered by Downtown Bridal.

Which will get more likes? The site focused on showing people what you are, or the site focused on how brides feel about themselves? Brides will want to connect with you when they know you get *them*.

Jeff: But what if I'm in a service business? What if my business isn't so much about products but about, for want of a better way to put it, me?

Shama: The same principle applies; in fact, when people are the focus it can be even more powerful.

That's why letting people connect with the CEO works so well. It's an extension of your brand. It's a relationship. Who would you rather connect with, a company or a person?

And that's why I resisted creating a page for our agency for a long time. I finally caved in when we decided to use it for customer service and answering questions. But it proves my point: I have over 200K Facebook subscribers, and our agency page has a few thousand. People like being able to connect with the CEO.

People want to connect with people. When you connect with a person at a business, it's like you know someone there. That's really powerful.

Jeff: Now put it into action. Tell me what to do.

Shama: The key is to forget what you want to say about yourself. Think about what your customers want to say and feel about themselves.

1. Start with your customers.

Forget *your* brand. What do your *customers* see as their brand?

Forget *your* messaging. What is the messaging of your *audience*?

For example, there's an Italian restaurant nearby. The interior is splashed with pictures of the owners, their families, and generations of people who have eaten there. They encourage customers to put their pictures up. When you walk in you instantly know they care about family, about tradition...you can tell family means everything to them.

People who care about family connect with the restaurant because it says something about how they see themselves.

Think in broader terms. How do your customers see themselves? What is important to them?

2. Create a platform that integrates your customers' brand with what you offer.

One of our clients runs chiropractic clinics. Many of their patients were injured in accidents. So they built a "don't text and drive" platform. They've created an entire campaign around preventing accidents. They frequently speak at schools and community events. They even created a pledge people can feature on their profiles to show it's something they care about. It's like bumper stickers on steroids.

The community cares about protecting their kids and, be honest, adults, because everyone is guilty of texting while they're driving. Our client cares about it, too. And they prove it.

Or take American Express: who would join a social network for a credit card company? No one. So Amex built Open Forum and created a community for small-business people who need information and resources. They do crazy numbers. If a credit card company can do it... you can, too.

Determine what you stand for, blend that with what your customers care about, and find the right balance point.

3. Be part of a movement.
Marketing has always been about you: your needs and your objectives.

Of course the goal is to get leads and sales, but with social media you should look at something bigger, become a part of a movement... be part of something your audience cares about.

Then you get more than bottom-line results: you get to be a part of something bigger and more meaningful.

The Dallas YMCA did a campaign featuring stories about their members and how the Y changed their life. In effect, they created a collage of beautiful stories and pictures. Those stories mean something to people. We all want to change our lives for the better and to be around people who feel the same way.

Bottom line: Don't mistake the medium for the message. That's not what it is.

Find a way to be of service—and to be a part of something bigger than your business.

"Facebook is a platform, a medium, and a killer app. It's contagious, infectious, and viral—but in the best meaning of those words."

Elliot Schrage,
Facebook.com

Facebook
King of the Social Media Jungle

Why Bother with Facebook?

- Facebook has more than 1.55 billion active monthly users and 1.31 billion active monthly mobile users, and it's growing every day.
- 91 percent of Millennials use Facebook.
- 34 percent of Facebook users are between the ages of 18 and 29.
- It offers fantastic online visibility for your brand.
- People are talking about you on there anyway. You may as well join in the conversation!

Facebook is like a coffee shop. Everyone is there for his or her own reasons, but it is a great place to strike up a conversation.

People from all walks of life use Facebook. They aren't there to buy stuff. They are there, first and foremost, to express themselves. After self-expression comes their need to connect with others.

Research shows that people use Facebook primarily to showcase their own identity—not just who they are but who they want to be perceived as. The friends we make, the groups we join, and the pages we "like" on Facebook are all offshoots of this basic identity creation and re-creation.

This is why you can never push products or services on Facebook. If you try to convert people directly to customers or clients, you will fail. However, if you are looking to attract consumers and build relationships over time, you will succeed. Your goal on Facebook should always be to attract people to your website, build trust, and gain visibility—all things that inevitably lead to sales.

How to Use Facebook

Facebook can be divided into five main parts: profiles (now also called timelines), pages, groups, events, and ads. Each part serves a certain function, and each has to be used uniquely.

Your profile is a way for you to present yourself to others. The main page of your profile is your own unique timeline. Over time, that timeline is populated by your life events, as well as a selection of updates and wall posts, organized by year. You cannot share a timeline.

Pages, short for fan pages, are for essentially anything and anyone that someone would care to be a fan of. Everything from Oreos to rock bands can have a page. Businesses and other entities have pages, not profiles, though pages also now use the timeline format.

Groups allow people to create subcommunities within Facebook around a topic of interest. There are serious groups, such as "Entrepreneurship," and silly ones like "I know what you did last summer."

Facebook events can be set up to attract participants to any live or virtual event.

Facebook advertising allows you to reach your target market based on their demographics and interests.

Facebook has gone from being just a social network for college students to a social center for people and businesses from all walks of life, and it has had to evolve to keep up. But although Facebook is constantly changing to keep up with demand, a lot of the basics remain the same.

Your Facebook Profile

This is where it all begins. Your Facebook profile is your personal space, your billboard, your calling card! A profile is *not* for businesses. A Facebook profile is for individuals only. Your profile is created automatically when you sign up for a Facebook account, and you will need a profile in order to join groups, add friends, generate ads, and create events.

If you are marketing your personal brand and don't mind the overlap of professional and personal, you can use your profile as a branding marketing tool. If you are marketing a business or a brand that you wish to keep separate from your personal network, you will want to focus on building a fan page. You can use your profile or your fan page (as we'll discuss later) to ATTRACT people initially, as well as intrigue them enough to visit your website (off of Facebook). You attract them by showcasing your expertise and sharing value.

Just keep in mind that Facebook pages have become much more robust than profiles over time in terms of marketing.

Status Updates (Your Timeline)

When you log in to Facebook, you are asked: "What's on your mind?" This is a very tricky question, because—let's face it—lots of thoughts run through our minds, and if we shared all of them, it would create a lot of noise. No one really cares if you just had breakfast, are getting an oil change, or just dropped off your kids at school.

Use the status updates in a strategic way. Share important business news, announce events, give advice, and provide *value*. Status updates are really the heart of Facebook because they create an ongoing impression of the person posting them. "Oh, Joe—he is such a partier. Just look at his Facebook updates!" "Jane—she is such a giver! She is constantly sharing tips with us." Share only when what you are doing matches your brand and provides value. In the following example, I mention that I am finishing up my book. This reminds people that I am writing a book; it builds curiosity! Plus, it's good information for anyone awaiting its release to have.

 Shama is putting the finishing touches on her book! a moment ago - clear

What are you doing right now?

Status updates are also great for starting conversations. You (and your friends) have the ability to comment on any status you post. It's a quick way to build stronger relationships.

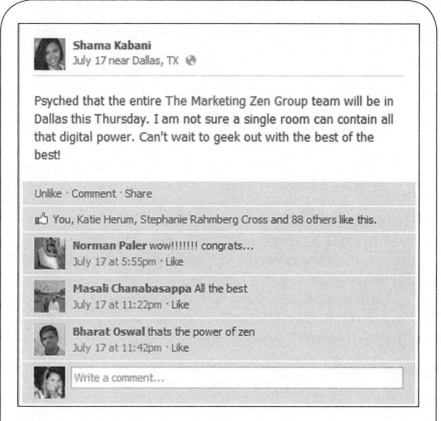

You can tag your friends, include your location, and determine exactly who sees the individual updates that you make. Once you click the update bar, you will see the features pictured here.

The following three stories illustrate how I have leveraged Facebook, using status updates, to further my business.

1. **Snagged a speaking engagement:** I posted that I was speaking at a local Dallas–Fort Worth event on Facebook marketing. Another local, Elizabeth Marshall, caught the update

and asked if I was willing to speak to her group on the same topic. I said yes, and we soon discovered that we were alums of the same high school—and even shared a favorite teacher! Liz and I have gone on to become good friends and have partnered on many occasions since.

2. **Received a press opportunity**: One day I got a phone call from a local TV station. They were doing a segment on Facebook and wanted to interview me. How did they know about me? A reporter from Austin had seen my updates on Facebook and knew I spoke on the topic. She'd given them my name.

3. **Established expertise**: When we succeeded in getting one of our client's keywords in the Google top ten, I posted an update about it. It was a great way to showcase our work because it established our expertise in the area and reminded people of what we can do. It also showcased my genuine excitement over our results.

About Section

The About section is where you want to showcase yourself in the best light. This section has six subsections: work and education, places you've lived, family and relationships, life events, details about you, and contact and basic info. You can choose to make certain aspects of the About section public or private. Whereas users tend to update everything else on Facebook fairly regularly, this area remains more or less the same—unless you change your favorite movies on a regular basis!

Fill out your About section as professionally and purposefully as possible. I can't stress this enough. Even though this is your personal profile, people will judge you professionally by it. This doesn't mean you can't have a life. By all means, share your interests and hobbies—but don't share anything that you wouldn't share with a stranger on the street.

Your profile information should be entered with a purpose in mind and reflect important events throughout your life—your life story. Are you going to use Facebook to attract more people to your business or are you going to use it to attract your next job? What do you want someone to walk away with after looking at your profile?

Did you know that lawyers can look up your Facebook profile and use it to *judge* whether you should be on a jury? Yes, the information you put up on Facebook can be used as evidence in a court of law. Furthermore, the FTC has ruled that companies can screen job applicants based on their internet photos and postings (that's everything from Facebook and Twitter to Flickr and blogs). In essence, what you decide to put online could determine your future.

Given that, you should fill out your About section as professionally as possible—even if you don't plan on using your personal profile for business. And don't share anything you would be embarrassed to find made public.

Facebook News Feed

Although not part of your profile, your Facebook news feed is unique to you and is the first thing you see when you log in to your account. It is the center column of your Facebook home page, and it constantly refreshes with a stream of updates (including links, pictures, and videos) from your Facebook friends and pages you like or subscribe to. Most people on Facebook don't visit profiles of their friends or visit the pages they like on a regular basis. They depend solely on the news feed.

How does Facebook determine what appears in your news feed? It bases it on an algorithm, much like Google or any other search engine does for search results. It uses factors such as how many of your friends commented on a story, who posted the story, what type of story it is (photo, video, or status update), and how much you interact with a particular friend or page. In addition to posts from friends and pages you follow, you will see tags, friend requests, event updates, group memberships, and other items reflecting your friends' Facebook activity as well as ads in the form of "sponsored posts." In short, it shows you news on what it calculates as being relevant to you rather than just what's recent.

If the marketer in you is wondering, "So, how can we end up on people's news feeds more?" that's an excellent question, and we will cover it momentarily. For now, I just want to make sure you're familiar with this terminology and setup.

Here is what my news feed looks like as I'm writing this:

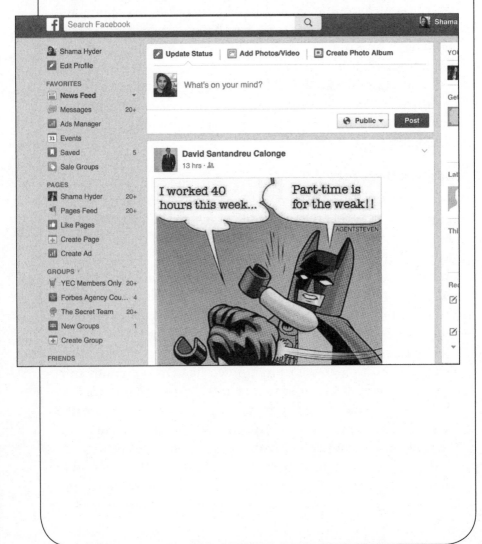

Facebook Privacy Settings

Facebook has created some very robust privacy settings, allowing you to decide who gets to view what part of your Facebook presence. For example, you may allow everyone to see your basic profile but only a select few to see your pictures. You can control those privacy settings by clicking on the "lock" icon on the top menu bar and then choosing Privacy Checkup from the drop-down menu. And as discussed previously, you can adjust the settings on individual status updates as well. The privacy settings control only general information; for everything else you can choose your audience each time you post.

A word of caution here: although you can certainly make things private, nothing is 100 percent secure. Facebook, after all, is just a website. It can experience glitches. If a glitch occurs and your private information is made public, make sure it isn't anything that would cause you embarrassment. Also keep in mind that your Facebook friends may share your information with others—intentionally or unintentionally. I personally know many people who let others, such as bosses or spouses, use their account to browse Facebook.

Again, never share anything—publicly or privately—that you wouldn't be comfortable sharing with a complete stranger.

How to Build Your Facebook Friendship Base

Does the number of friends you have matter? Yes, to a degree. Does this mean you should obsess over building your numbers? No. Having more friends is great because it means you have a bigger pool to network with. You can use Facebook to keep up with current customers and vendors, and you can also use it to meet new people. But a lot of people get stuck on the word "friends" and equate their friend number with their worth. It totally depends on how you wish to define a "Facebook friend." Remember that on Facebook, "friend" may just mean someone you know.

Facebook now allows people to subscribe to your updates

rather than be your friend. It also allows people who subscribe to you to repost your update to their own network, beyond your friends and subscribers. When they repost, subscribers help spread your personal and professional brand.

You do want to focus on having a high-quality group to network with. Let's look at four ways you can start building a quality base of both friends and subscribers.

1. **Use the tools that Facebook provides when you first create an account.** One tool will look through your email address book to see who in it is already using Facebook. This is a quick way to find people you already know. You can send a friend request to anyone you want, but start with good friends and colleagues so you can start to build your network fast. Also, don't be surprised if the first time you log on, you see friend requests waiting for you to approve. More people than you realize may already be on Facebook and looking for you!

2. **Bring offline networking online.** When you go to conferences or mixers and bring home a stack of business cards, search for those people on Facebook and add them as friends. Then throw away their cards! Facebook will even remind you of their birthdays.

3. **Register your Facebook username.** Facebook allows each profile to have an easy username and custom URL. You can go to www.facebook.com/username to set up your own username. This makes it very easy for you to share your profile with others.

4. **Allow subscribers.** From your personal timeline, click the subscribers tab on the left menu, underneath the cover photo. This will allow you to post public updates and allow people outside of your network of friends to read them. Your subscribers will see only the updates that you make public. If you wish to share something only with friends, you can.

Marketing with social media has created an equal, level playing field for this new era in business. It has given personal brands an opportunity to compete with big brands. Entrepreneurs don't have to have a big budget or a lot of capital to position themselves as a thought leader in their industry. As someone who started without a big following, database, or big budget, marketing with social media gave me the chance to position myself as an authority in the marketing arena. Now anyone with a passion and a message can do the same thing and build a loyal tribe.

Alejandro Reyes,
Successfool.com

Facebook Groups

Facebook groups work really well for currently existing offline or other online groups. For example, you can set up a group for your company, your college reunion planning committee, or even your CEO breakfast group. You can keep your group open to the public, closed (anyone can see that the group exists if they search for it, but only members can access and see posts), or even secret (invite-only and can't be found in searches). Groups don't work so well when you are trying to market a product or build brand awareness. Do not create a group around your brand or business. This is what (as we will soon discuss) pages are for.

Groups are very much like online forums—a modern equivalent of a traditional bulletin board. They're a place where users generate content, host discussions, and create a community of sorts. On Facebook, the owner of a group serves as its moderator.

They are a fabulous way to create your community for free. You can find groups by clicking on the Groups icon (on the left side of the bottom menu bar). You can go to www.facebook.com/groups to search and create groups. You can also invite friends to join your group. A person doesn't have to be your Facebook friend to join your group, but you can (and should) invite friends you think would be interested to join. You don't want to invite people blindly, however. Let's say you want to set up a Facebook group for your son's school's PTA. You want to specifically invite those friends whom you know are part of the PTA. There is one huge drawback of groups—less for the creator and more for the members. It works based on an opt-out system versus an opt-in one. That means you can add any friend to a group; he or she doesn't have to give you consent first. Then, if that friend chooses not be a part of it, he or she can leave—an opt-out system. Facebook may change this eventually. For now, you want to be careful when you add people to a group. Be sure that you have their consent or know that they would truly want to be a part of the group before you add them.

On the following page is a group that I belong to—offline and online. It is called the Young Entrepreneur Council, and it's made up of young entrepreneurs who support each other in their ventures and work to reduce youth unemployment.

What all can you do with Facebook groups?

- Connect and network with other like-minded individuals.
- Provide a convenient place for your current network to meet and stay connected.
- Provide value and increase visibility within your current group.
- Post relevant pictures and videos. This provides content as well as helps your group members feel like they are part of the community.

Facebook Pages

Facebook pages, or fan pages, as they are sometimes called, were created in late 2007 because Facebook wanted to give businesses a space for their brands but didn't want businesses to create profiles, which Facebook reserved for people. If Facebook finds that a business has created a profile instead of a page, they will close the account. This is why you should keep your profiles personal and create a *page* for your business.

Pages are much more customizable than groups. The best part is that pages are indexed by Google. By default, all fan pages are public. That means if someone searches for your company or for keywords that you cover in your page, your page will show up in Google's search results. This is an easy step toward search engine optimization.

If you are looking to build a brand and market your company, you will want a fan page, hands down. You will notice that fan pages have switched over to the timeline format, much like the personal profiles. Despite this, pages still have different functions/uses.

Because pages have recently adopted the timeline change, they can now have a unique cover photo and take advantage of several other new features. These new features may come with a few drawbacks for businesses, however. There are certain rules and regulations your brand will need to follow once it adopts the timeline format.

What Is the Difference Between a Personal Profile and a Fan Page? Can You Have Both?

Facebook offers profiles and pages. A profile is meant for individuals. A page can also be for an individual, but any entity (a business, a nonprofit, a dog) can also set up a page. The original idea was that profiles allowed you to connect with people you knew, like your friends, while a page allowed you to connect with a greater audience. Anyone who wanted to get your updates could "like" a page. However, with the launch of the timeline feature, Facebook also added a new feature to personal profiles—the Follow feature. Now, if you allow it, people can subscribe to your profile. Anyone who "follows" your profile can see anything that you have made public. And your information shows up in their Facebook news feeds. Following and friending are exclusive of each other. You can follow someone's profile without becoming their friend. And even if you friend someone on Facebook, you can unsubscribe to their updates.

The question becomes: Do you now need both—a profile and a page? If your company wants a presence on Facebook, a page is still the best option. However, if you are an individual, you can choose to have a profile, which allows subscribers versus having a page. The upside to this is that you have to manage only one account. The downside is that you cannot market or advertise to your subscribers as you can to fans of your page. At least not yet.

I resisted creating a page for The Marketing Zen Group officially for a long time. As the CEO, I wanted people to be able to connect with me personally. However, people started "liking" The Marketing Zen Group without us even setting up a page for it. After 50 likes, it was obvious that the people had spoken. They wanted us to have a presence on Facebook. So we "claimed" the company, and now have an official company fan page as well. You can visit it at www.facebook.com/MarketingZenGroup.

Here is my personal profile:

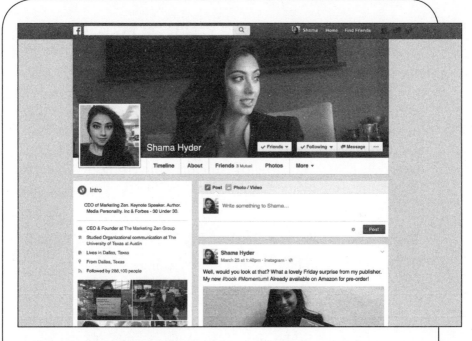

Here is our company's fan page:

What If I Already Have a Profile for My Business with a Large Following?

Not to worry—Facebook has a tool that will convert your business profile to a page for you! Go to www.facebook.com/pages/create.migrate and you can complete the transition. You will go through the basic steps for creating a page, and then Facebook will port over your photos and transform your friends into fans. Facebook does not currently support converting a profile to an existing page or merging multiple profiles, pages, or places, however.

What Should Be the Goal of My Facebook Fan Page?

Ideally, you should be focused on three things:

1. **Building up your fan base**. This comes by way of "likes." If someone "likes" your page, they are considered a fan. Did you know that the average annualized value of a Facebook fan is $136.38? That number includes product spending, brand loyalty, propensity to recommend, and many other factors (which vary by industry).

2. **Keeping interaction consistent and high**. Unfortunately, due to algorithm changes aimed at marketers and businesses, most of your Facebook fans will never see your posts in their news feeds unless you pay to promote them. While a pay-to-play model is understandably annoying, it does have some upsides. As I'll explain in a later chapter, paid Facebook advertising is more targeted and effective than ever before—if you post the right kind of content to get your audience engaged and interacting with you. Some kinds of posts naturally receive more interaction than others. Photo albums, pictures, and videos receive 180 percent, 120 percent, and 100 percent more engagement respectively.

3. **Driving traffic and leads to your website**. Remember, Facebook is a tool to attract!

How to Promote Your Facebook Page

You should be using every tool in your toolbox to promote your Facebook page at its inception (and throughout your entire social media journey).

Hit the Ground Running

Begin by sending a designated email blast to the current clients in your email database. Send an internal email instructing employees to like your page and recommend the page to their friends and family members.

To do so, they go to your Facebook page, click the Settings icon next to the "Message" button, and scroll down to click "Share." Employ your current customers as your brand ambassadors and ask them to help spread the word about your new page.

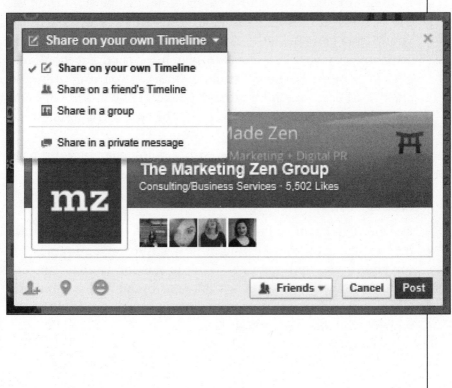

You can select a username for your page, just like you can for your personal profile. To do this, follow the same instructions given in the profile section of this chapter. Make sure to check your spelling because you can edit it only once after it is created!

If you have a physical location associated with your brand (or multiple franchises, offices, etc.), use traditional signage to notify customers that you are joining the Facebook world. Incorporate QR codes into the creative design on each poster or tabletop to connect instantly with smartphone users.

You can also set your business up as a place and offer exclusive items to consumers when they check in to encourage them to connect with you. The best part? You get free social advertising when the update is sent out to their Facebook friends that they checked in at your page!

To set up your place on Facebook, you must be at your physical location. On a smartphone, go to Nearby Places. Search for your listing and click "Check In" (a customer may have already set it up, in which case you can search for it on Facebook and click "Claim my business" at the bottom). If you cannot find it, click "Add new" and fill out the details. When you add your correct address to your Facebook page, the two will automatically sync up.

Once you get to 200 fans, you cannot change your page name, so make sure your choice is well thought out!

Posting Basics

Beyond that, having a firm social media policy and/or guidelines in place helps to keep posting orderly, approved, and representing your brand appropriately. What to post on your fan page—and when and how—depends on your brand and company. It also depends on how your customers want to interact with you, which is the most important thing.

AHA! Zen Moment

POSTING Q&A

From a report in Momentous Media:

1. *When is the best time to post?*
   answer: Weekends and off-peak hours
2. *How many times should I post per day?*
   answer: As many times as you want
3. *What type of content elicits the most interaction?*
   answer: #1 Photos, #2 Statuses
4. *Should I ask fans to Like and Comment on my posts?*
   answer: Yes! Asking to Like increases interaction 216 percent.
5. *Should I ask my fans questions?*
   answer: Questions don't increase the interaction rate, but they do increase commenting rate. Make sure to ask fans to answer your questions with a comment.
6. *How long should my status messages be?*
   answer: Long or short, we found no correlation between length and interaction rate. ⚱

Don't be afraid to step outside of the box with your posting. If you post a link every day to your website (unless you have a very dynamic, robust site), your audience is going to get bored. There is nothing wrong with posting about current events; in fact, most times they spark more interaction. Just be careful not to impose your own opinion. For instance, baked goods company Entenmann's faced backlash on Twitter when they used the #notguilty hashtag made popular by the Casey Anthony trial. A Twitter uproar started, and Entenmann's was very quick to apologize, admitting they didn't know what the hashtag referenced. The same goes for Facebook. Be mindful of what you are saying, what you are posting, and what your audience may say or do in response.

Here are a few ideas for content generation:

- Blog posts
- Quotes (people love to "like" quotes)
- Questions about people's lives
- Questions about holiday plans
- Exciting company breakthroughs/happenings
- Employee spotlights or anything personal (especially with larger brands where people aren't expecting this type of transparency—surprise them!)
- Comments on current events
- Articles related to your industry
- Funny facts related to your product or service
- Shout-outs to communities your brand interacts with
- Local or national stories of goodwill
- Videos and photos

Videos and images are hands down some of the very best types of content for garnering engagement and interaction from your audience, so you'll want to make them an important part of your Facebook strategy.

Using the Timeline to Promote Your Brand

There are several features that come with the timeline format that are useful for promotion—especially since the timeline is the first thing new visitors see.

1. **Pin your post.** You can now pin important posts to the top of your timeline for up to seven days. (You can do this up to three days after the original post is made.)
2. **Set brand milestones.** For example, launching a new product, winning awards, or opening a new store. Don't limit yourself to current milestones; with the timeline feature you can go back and add milestones to the company history. These appear highlighted on your timeline.

3. **Add a unique cover photo**. Your cover photo is a great way to help your fans visualize your brand. There are, however, limitations. You cannot include purchase info or sales, contact information (website, address, phone), or calls to action ("like us," "get it now").

4. **Promote your post**. Promoted posts are one of Facebook's most effective ad formats. Each post has its own set of analytics, called "insights," that allows you to see how many fans it reached. Promoting important posts is also one of the best ways to reach your audience, since Facebook no longer displays business page posts in fans' news feeds.

Campaigns and Contests

We encourage our clients to launch some sort of campaign or contest relating to their brand in an effort to draw in new fans and to keep current fans coming back to the page to connect. Offer all your fans a discount of some sort, offer a free product or service, or give away a fun new piece of technology. Larger or more exclusive prizes yield higher entrance rates, but try to use something that relates to your brand.

The less information or work that is required on the entrant's part, the more likely people are to actually enter. Be sure to collect an email address (so that you can contact the winner), but if you intend to use it for anything else, you must notify entrants. Also, be sure to have an extensive list of rules (you can put this in your notes section on your page) outlining your rights to use their submitted content, age requirements, state laws, or whatever applies to your campaign.

Here are a few ways to share your contest or campaign:

- Use Facebook Advertising (see Chapter 10)
- Reach out to bloggers in your industry to help spread the word
- Send a designated email blast to your current database

- Share the contest on Twitter, YouTube, and any other channels your brand uses
- Post signage about the campaign at your physical location
- Promote your contest posts to encourage maximum visibility within your current network
- Have staff personally encourage clients to enter

Be prepared to lose a few fans at the end of your contest, as "like 'em and leave 'em" Facebook users do exist. And if you have a campaign in which you select a winner personally, be prepared for user backlash. Though you may not always have to combat this, contests where users select a winner or where one is chosen at random leave less room for speculation about playing favorites or fixed results.

Most importantly, be sure to read up on Facebook's everchanging promotions guidelines to make sure your contest complies (Facebook has the power to ban certain pages because of noncompliance). Watch for updates here: www.facebook.com/promotions_guidelines.php.

Facebook Events

Facebook events are a great way to promote any event or milestone, and also provide a channel for direct communication with your fans through event "attendance." It doesn't even have to be a physical event. Virtual events like teleseminars, webinars, and even reminders to enter a contest also qualify.

When you create a Facebook event, you get a full page featuring your event (which looks much like a group or page).

As it does with pages, Facebook allows indexing of public events. This means SEO benefits for you! You can choose to show the attendees or not, make the event public or private, and customize your message entirely.

What kinds of events can you promote?

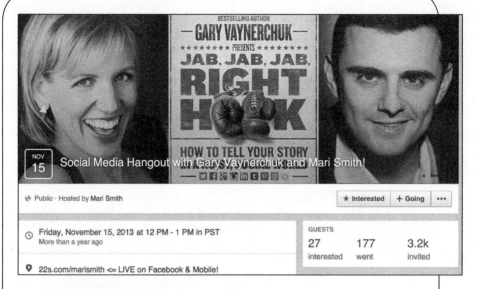

NOV
15 Social Media Hangout with Gary Vaynerchuk and Mari Smith!

Public · Hosted by **Mari Smith**

★ Interested   + Going   •••

🕐 Friday, November 15, 2013 at 12 PM - 1 PM in PST
More than a year ago

GUESTS		
27	177	3.2k
interested	went	invited

📍 22s.com/marismith <= LIVE on Facebook & Mobile!

- Local live events
- Live events in other cities
- Contests/campaigns
- Performances
- Book signings
- Teleseminars/webinars
- Virtual events
- Product launches
- New store openings
- Nonprofit events (walks, benefits, etc.)
- Parties
- Educational classes
- Meetings (formal or informal)

How to Create an Event on Facebook

Go to your brand's Facebook page, click on the "More" tab under the profile picture, and then click "Events." You will be presented with a simple form, like the one on the next page, to fill out. Note that you can host an event personally or host through a group you moderate.

Keys to Promoting Your Event on Facebook

Follow these six guidelines:

1. **Choose a catchy title.** I get at least five event requests a day. I look at only the ones that catch my eye.
2. **Create a clear and thorough description**. It's annoying to see one-liners. "Join Us" isn't a description. Show people what's in it for them.

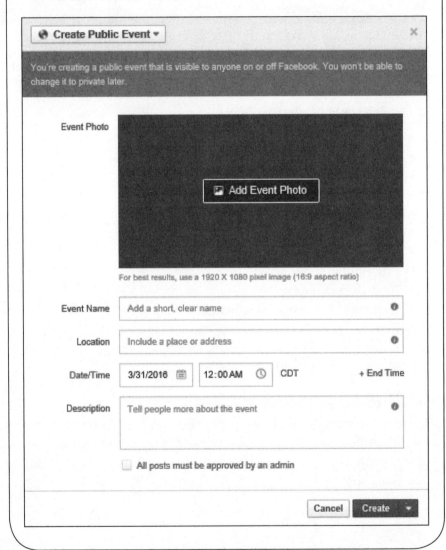

3. **Include time zones.** Facebook has users on every continent—including Antarctica. Remember to select the appropriate time zone in the description area.
4. **Invite your guests to bring their friends.** You want to get the word out, right? Encourage your friends to invite other friends. But...
5. **Don't invite blindly.** Spend some time thinking about who might benefit by attending. Add this to your description: "You are being invited because..." Also, note that you can no longer invite fans from the page itself. You can only post the event on the timeline. Admins must invite using their personal accounts.
6. **Post pictures and video.** Did you host the same event last year? Share those pictures! Give people something that will help them get a feel for the event.

About Facebook Applications

Ever been bitten by a zombie or been invited to a Criminal Case game? Ever raised virtual farm animals on Facebook? If so, you've interacted with an application, or "app" as they are better known. Applications are also what allow you to take quizzes like "Which *Friends* Character Are You?" As Facebook evolves, Facebook applications will continue to gain popularity and visibility. Most applications aren't developed by Facebook but by outside companies.

Can You Use Applications as a Marketing Tool?

Yes! Applications are a great way for brands to interact and give back to their fans, especially if they have very specific tie-ins to the product. This Dunkin' Donuts app is very popular because when people connect to it in order to play a game, their points go toward their Dunkin' purchases.

One fairly successful application is the Schweppes "Profile App," which allows users to take one image and crop it to fit across their five photo series. I used this and at least fifty people asked me about it and ended up using it within the first week.

Facebook now requires pages to host contests on third-party applications such as Shortstack, OfferPop, or Wildfire (see more that follows). Once activated, these applications are then featured under your page's main profile image. They are easy to share and

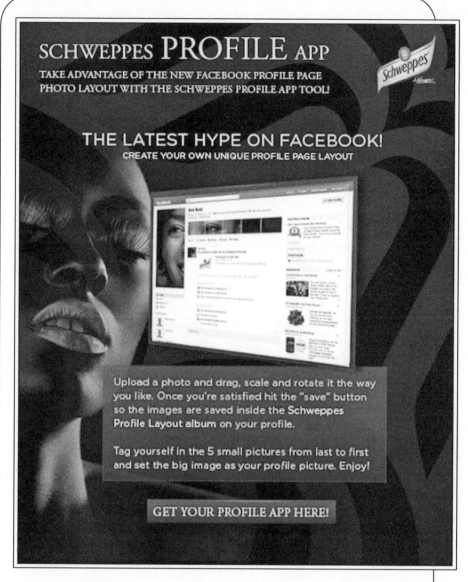

can support any feature of your contest or campaign. Refer to the Campaigns and Contests section for more information.

Facebook Commerce Applications

Applications can also lend themselves to greater integration between businesses and Facebook. An early adopter of this deep integration was 1-800-Flowers.com.

For 1-800-Flowers, recurring events drive recurring revenue. Its potential customers have real needs that can be used to drive sales, and by integrating with Facebook, 1-800-Flowers can target these customers more effectively—using holidays, special occasions, and also significant dates for those in an individual's network, such as birthdays.

The managers of 1-800-Flowers use Facebook Connect, giving users the ability to log on to their 1-800-Flowers account with their Facebook log on. The integration of the two platforms not only gives 1-800-Flowers access to users' networks but also makes it much easier for users to create a profile on 1-800-Flowers.com.

Technology also provides a way to bridge the gap between the average person's busy lifestyle and the basic need to give gifts to those close to them on special occasions. Most Facebook users have their birthdays connected to their personal profiles, so letting 1-800-Flowers remember for them decreases the chance of users forgetting an important one.

Most companies are not the size of 1-800-Flowers, but the takeaway from this solution is the focus on convenience: convenience in logging on with Facebook Connect, convenience in setting up reminders for gift-giving occasions, and convenience in purchasing and sending the gift. The value proposition to the user is really less about the product and more about the convenience.

Albert Maruggi,
Founder and President of ProvidentPartners.net

What About Adding Applications on Your Page?

Each brand and industry benefits from different apps. An art gallery may benefit from simple Facebook apps like Photos and Videos, whereas a restaurant chain may benefit from a personalized online ordering application. You can edit what apps are visible on your timeline by clicking on the right-hand corner of each one under the cover photo. By then clicking the pencil icon, you can swap positions, edit the app, or remove it.

If you're considering creating an app, the trick is to make one that is enticing enough that users will be willing to connect with it, thereby relinquishing their personal information. As your app becomes an important part of how users express themselves, their app-related actions are more prominently displayed throughout the timeline, news feed, and ticker, thus reaching their friend network and giving your company more visibility.

A directory of applications can be found at www.facebook .com/apps.

Facebook Open Graph

Facebook Connect is being replaced by Open Graph as a means for sharing web content while being connected to your personal profile. Just as Facebook Connect allowed users to "like" certain content or comment on blogs as their Facebook profile and share the activity on their wall, Open Graph aims to make all web content "likeable," "shareable," and available for commenting. After a user adds the app, app-specific actions are shared on Facebook via Open Graph.

In short, Open Graph allows users to "connect" their Facebook identity, friends, and settings to any website. If you have ever commented on a blog, you probably had to provide your name, email address, and website URL. Now if a website has Facebook Open Graph in place, you can simply log in to the website using your Facebook ID. As a website owner, you definitely want to have Facebook Open Graph set up on your website. It takes some technical savvy, but you can find all the directions at devel opers.facebook.com/docs/opengraph. Now, not only can visitors to your website log in using their Facebook ID, but you can see exactly who is visiting your website. And when they comment on your blog, it shows on their profile for all their friends to see as well. This means that as a brand all your products and services will have that much more of a chance of being recognized individually. Your online visibility is amplified.

Facebook Do's and Don'ts for Brands

DO:

- ✓ Spend time creating an outstanding timeline with cover photo.
- ✓ Let your brand's voice and personality shine through and be consistent.
- ✓ Reach out to people consistently, *truly* engaging with them.
- ✓ Build a loyal Facebook fan base and thank/flatter them frequently.
- ✓ Leverage your page's posts and status updates by providing value.
- ✓ Make use of the timeline features: scheduling posts, pinning posts, featuring posts, and promoting posts.
- ✓ Work on attracting people to your site (using real value, not pushy links).
- ✓ Have a commenting policy in place to set page expectations.
- ✓ Build a community around your topic or specialty.
- ✓ Be proactive in intercepting and responding to feedback, positive or negative.
- ✓ Share relevant pictures and videos.
- ✓ Participate actively in conversations, but let "the people" speak!

DON'T:

- ☒ Be pushy.
- ☒ Post the same content repeatedly . . . yes, that is spam.
- ☒ Delete or leave idle negative feedback.
- ☒ Use multiple voices without notifying users with a signature or handle.
- ☒ Put up crude or thoughtless pictures or comments.
- ☒ Expect social media to "work" for you (you have to work it!).
- ☒ Be impatient (real relationships take time to build).
- ☒ Let feedback go unnoticed. Watch your stats, know where to improve, and work hard to find the right recipe for success daily!

How Should You ACT on Facebook?

Attract: As cliché as it sounds, provide value to your users. Why would they like you, let alone come back to your page daily to interact with you if you don't?

Convert: You may not gain clients directly from Facebook, but you can gain consumers. Remember the value of each of those Facebook fans. If you keep them happy, they *will* bring you their business.

Transform: Facebook is a powerful platform to showcase your desire for a real relationship with your users. Your brand should profit while the consumer feels *great* about it! Have fun with it! 🧘

How to Be Proactive on Facebook

You should take the following actions *daily* on Facebook:

- Check your page for any posts (negative or positive) that need a response.
- Post or prepare content (comment on other pages, find relevant timely news to post, etc.).
- Urge your users to comment, like, or share something.
- Check any campaigns, applications, or inquiries, and tend to them.

Take the following actions *weekly:*

- Post new photos of an event, a day at the office, or something funny for users to comment on.
- Post a new video from your series if you have one or a relevant video in your industry to capture users' attention.

- Provide a link to your website (your blog, or other useful information) or other social media account (company LinkedIn page, Twitter account, etc.)—but only if for a notable reason.

Take the following actions *monthly:*

- Track how many people visited your website from Facebook and measure which articles or posted links got the most feedback. Then do more of what works!
- Strategize your content calendars, campaigns, and initiatives for the coming month, and get creative needs handled, so that you can monitor your page stress-free.

A Cautionary Note

I would be remiss if I didn't add the following warning. As you build your community on Facebook, be sure to drive it outward—to your website, your email list, and so on. Why? Because as much as you feel that you own your own brand's information and contacts on a social media site, you don't. If Facebook ever decides to ban your account (and I have seen it done, even to people who always followed the rules), you don't want to be stranded.

There is a service, digi.me, which will back up your profile, pictures, and a list of your friends. This is a very worthwhile investment. But even if you have this backup in place, I reiterate: Use Facebook as a tool to attract, but constantly look to pull people to your site.

Facebook fan pages were created to be the official presence on Facebook for companies, nonprofits, and celebrities. Fan pages provide an incredibly rich opportunity for small and large businesses to interact with customers and fans, and find new customers and fans. You can think of fan pages as microsites . . . [They] feature Facebook applications such as Photos, Videos, Events, Reviews, and Notes, and even applications customized just for your company.

However, the major advantage of Facebook fan pages over microsites or your own company websites is that they are built on the Facebook platform—where a lot of people are spending a lot of time each day. To be precise, as of September 2009, 300 million users are on Facebook, with 1 million new users per day! Furthermore, Facebook ads allow you to "hypertarget" based on demographic information and keyword information found in profiles—not only to find out how many people in your particular target audience are on Facebook, but to reach them and draw them over to your fan page. For example, an Italian restaurant in Cleveland can choose to advertise only to men and women ages twenty-five to forty who list "Italian food" as an interest. A Dallas florist can choose to advertise only to women within a twenty-five-mile radius of Dallas who list themselves as "engaged." Once people become "fans" of your page, you can interact with them on a regular basis, just as you would interact with your friends.

No matter what your business or organization, chances are now that your customers and potential customers are using Facebook. Why not bring your business to them?

Dave Kerpen,
Chief Buzz Officer of Likeable Media (www.likeable.com)

> "Twitter is an online social networking service and microblogging service that enables its users to send and read text-based posts of up to 140 characters, known as 'tweets.'"
>
> Wikipedia

Twitter
Conversation, Engagement, and Sharing

Why Bother with Twitter?

- It has over 300 million monthly active users as of 2012 and around an estimated billion registered users.
- 23 percent of all adult internet users are on Twitter.
- 37 percent of people between 18 and 29, 25 percent of those between 30 and 49, 12 percent of those between 50 and 64, and 10 percent of those 65 and older are using Twitter.
- It provides excellent online visibility.
- It's a great way to attract traffic.
- It allows for instant communication.

Twitter is like a giant, colorful bazaar where you can attract attention and create an expert platform like never before. People use Twitter not just to connect with one another, but to share what they need, so it's *much* easier to spot people who might need your help on Twitter than it is on Facebook.

Twitter Basics

Let's start with some basic Twitter knowledge.

You get 140 characters to answer: "What's happening?" This is the entire premise of Twitter. However, the worst thing you can do is *actually* answer that question. (I will get to that in a bit!)

Messages that people send out are called "tweets." "Tweeting" is another common phrase; it means sending a message via Twitter. Your tweets make up a timeline. When people subscribe to your timeline, or "follow" you, your tweets show up on their Twitter home page. These people are called followers. You can follow them back if you choose. Unlike Facebook, following does not have to be mutual. You can follow anyone you want, but they don't have to follow you back.

Everyone gets a Twitter name, also known as a "handle." Choose one that's short and memorable. You can thank me for this later when your followers are able to retweet your messages more easily.

You don't have to reply to all tweets. If you want to reply to someone's tweets or want to get someone's attention, type @username and then your message. For example, let's say you want to tweet me. Currently I have over 25,000 followers, and only 10 messages or so show up on my home page. If you want to get on my radar, it is most effective to tweet "at" me: @Shama.

Your home page defaults to your timeline, which shows a random assortment (chronologically) of messages tweeted by the people you are following. The following image shows my home page. When someone sends you an "@" reply, it will show up on your home page and will also be filed under the @Connect tab at the top of your home page.

You can also send direct messages to people. The 140-character limit still applies, and you can send only direct messages to people who are following you. This isn't the same as sending replies, which can be sent to anyone using the @ sign. Direct messages are hidden from public view and shown only to the recipient. To send someone a message directly, click the icon to the right of the search bar and select "Message" on the left, underneath their profile. This will open a window that allows you to type in your message.

You don't have to use your browser to get on Twitter. You can use a desktop application. My favorite is TweetDeck, an app so successful Twitter acquired it (www.TweetDeck.com). There are also tons of mobile applications for Twitter. Just search the internet for "Twitter application + [device of your choice]" (e.g., Mac, iPad, Android, etc.).

Many Twitter users use hashtags, words that include the hash symbol (#), to keep relevant tweets organized. Hashtags were developed by the Twitter community to make it easier to search for relevant tweets. They are very popular at conferences and seminars, where many people might be twittering, because they make it easy to track what is going on at an event.

For example, during the Iranian elections, a lot of Twitter users were updating Twitter with news. They would use the hashtag #iran or #irannews, so if someone was searching for tweets on this topic, he or she could find them easily.

It's All About the Dialogue!

Although most of my friends consider me an early adopter, everything I get involved with already has at least a sprinkling of users, so I think I'm somewhere closer to the middle. Nonetheless, in the case of Twitter, I've had an account since it was a weird, unknown service with a funny name, long before Oprah and Ashton Kutcher created the race for followers and wayyy long before TV shows decided that a Twitter crawl on the bottom of the screen offered pretensions of interactivity.

Heck, in the old days, having more than 500 followers was an amazing feat, and those people who got into the four-digit follower numbers were the wizened elite, the really popular folk on the service. Now there are so many (spammy) tools to garner followers (none of whom are actually paying any attention to you) that it's common to see newbies who have thousands of followers and no clue how Twitter works.

Twitter certainly can be a one-way communication channel, a 140-character megaphone to an audience of thousands, but to do that is to miss out on what differentiates Twitter from the many other social media services available: it's interactive and lets you instantly *establish a dialogue* with your customers and community.

I know Shama gets this, but I worry that you, the reader, might not. Please, to really understand the value of Twitter and to really gain benefit from your involvement, keep in mind that you need to *give more than you expect to receive.* Don't ask, "How many followers can I blast my message to?" but instead, "How many people can I engage in a dialogue with?"

You'll be surprised just how much more enjoyable—and valuable—the experience will be.

Dave Taylor,
DaveTaylorOnline.com

Another major example of global hashtag usage was #London2012 and #Olympics. The Olympics were especially popular on Twitter, as a great number of the athletes who participated had their own Twitter accounts. Brands, businesses, media outlets, and fans from countries all around the world could monitor and keep tabs on the event happenings in real time, as well as interact with other Twitter users interested in the subject.

If you will be attending a trade show or any other type of event later in the year, find out if a hashtag is being used specifically for the event and interact before, during, and after the event. By doing this, you will maximize your networking time and learn from the community where you will need to focus your time at the event.

You can see current hashtags at hashtags.org or use Twitter's search feature to see if any of the hashtags you think should exist actually do exist. Many industries have their own hashtags—e.g., #slpeeps (speech pathologists) and #eventprofs (event planning professionals)—so it is also a good way for both B2C and B2B businesses to find their audiences and start engaging. Hashtags can also be used ironically or as commentary to add color.

Retweeting (RT) is reposting another person's tweet. This can have a quick viral effect when the quality of the information is good. For example, let's say you post a link from your blog. If I am following you and I like the link, I will retweet it to my followers. An icon below each tweet allows you to easily retweet it, providing the option to add a comment of your own in the process. In addition, there are also two widely used formats for manually retweeting:

- Type "RT @username" and then copy and paste their message.
- Copy and paste their message followed by "(via @username)."

When retweeting (the word retweet is now in the Oxford English Dictionary), take the time to write a personal note about why you are retweeting this information. Respond and the user who you are retweeting may reply back to you with a mention. When anyone mentions you, your reach expands in the best way—it means someone is advocating for you/your Twitter name, and their followers may begin to follow you, too.

Your Personal Twitter Page

Your Twitter experience starts with your Twitter page or personal profile. This is different from your profile on Facebook because it gives you less room to play with. You have to be succinct on Twitter. The following tips can help you make the most of your Twitter profile.

- Start by picking a short username. Ideally, go with your first name. Although Twitter allows you to use business names as handles, I recommend you go with your personal name. People want to be friends with people. If you are a big company looking to further your brand and provide customer service on Twitter, use your company name. If you have multiple employees using Twitter, you can create a cohandle—a handle that incorporates both the individual's name and the company's. For example, Mike-Nike and SteveCEO-Nike are cohandles.

- Use a good headshot. You don't get much space for a picture, so make sure it is large and clear and captures attention.

- The same applies to your bio. You get 160 characters for it, so be concise and direct. This isn't the place to be vague or wordy. Focus on what you do and/or who you help. Mine says: "Founder and CEO of Marketing Zen. Keynote Speaker. Author. Media Personality. Globe Trotter. Go-Getter. Inc & Forbes - 30 Under 30." I could also say: "Helping businesses leverage the internet as president of The Marketing Zen Group."

- You get one web address. If you have multiple websites or multiple businesses, pick one to showcase here. I choose to showcase Shama.TV because it allows people to get to know me as a person better, and because I point out my business URL in my bio.

- Get and use a personalized header photo. Everyone who visits your profile can see it. You can see mine at www.twitter.com/Shama. Any graphic designer can create one for you. We create them on occasion for our clients as well. Why? It's a great marketing tool, and it will set you apart! You don't get

The main purpose of marketing in any institution is to tell the story behind the brand. How do you connect well with your customers in order to sell your product or service? Twitter is a great tool to use in order to show that "personality" behind a company or a brand. Use Twitter to drive people (traffic) to a blog that tells your story. Talk about your customers, clients, and your business. Twitter is a great avenue to connect with customers on a personal level, as well as on a professional level. Use it to your advantage.

Kyle Lacy,
author of Twitter Marketing for Dummies

to say a lot using your 160-character bio, but you can make a great impression using your header photo. Make sure it includes your name, a way to reach you (email, phone, or both), your major websites, and a brief bio. Keep it clutter free, use your brand colors, and again, be succinct!

Who to Follow

On Twitter, you can choose to follow everyone you find and amass diverse tweets or you can choose to follow a specific few from whom you derive value. I follow a variety of people, and it makes for a very robust Twitter experience. If you are interested in someone's tweets, follow him or her. Don't worry about whether he or she follows you back. You will attract your own group of followers.

Here are a few tips to get started:

- Upload your contact list, and see who is already on Twitter. You may be surprised. To do this, click on the #Discover tab, and select "Search Contacts" next to the email provider that you use.
- Look for more people you know. Twitter has a search tool that allows you to search for people using keywords and names.
- Feel free to follow me (@Shama). I will follow back. (My open-door policy applies on Twitter as well!)

- If you belong to another social media site, announce that you are now on Twitter. Be sure to give your username. Status updates on Facebook and LinkedIn are a great way to make announcements like this.
- Once you have at least five followers, look at who they follow. If they seem interesting, follow them.
- Use Twellow.com and Moz's FollowerWonk.com, directories of people on Twitter organized by industry and interest. You can look for people to follow and list yourself as well. For example, if you are a PR pro, you'd want to look for reporters so that if they need a source for a story, you are there. Follow people within niches: industry, city, occupation, and so on. It is a great way to meet locals.
- Check to see if your favorite bloggers, actors, or media personalities are on Twitter. Chances are, they are. Follow them. Often they are easier to get in touch with via Twitter because it only takes them a few characters to respond.
- See who the people you follow recommend. I often recommend good people to follow. There is a current trend on Twitter called Follow Friday. Twitterers recommend who they follow to their followers followed by the #followfriday or #ff hashtag on Fridays. (You follow?)

Marketing via Twitter represents a very unique and compelling channel for marketers. Its ease of use, transactional speed, pure text format, and ability to reach a large audience in 140 characters offers simplicity and yet complexity. For big brands, the ability to connect directly with consumers offers a free fall of both good and bad feedback, and many are using Twitter as a customer service channel. Furthermore, for transactional products, a very compelling promotion can get unbelievable reach and offer a potential viral impact. For individuals, social media influence is driven by content and relationships. Many have built strong personal brands with Twitter by sharing and creating content and engaging individuals and companies.

Mike D. Merrill,
MikeMerrill.com

How to Make the Most of Twitter

Think of Twitter as a global human search engine. It is completely what you make of it.

Let me give you an example. I was scheduled to speak to a group of CEOs at an organization called Vistage that I had never spoken to before. The group's host had forewarned me that this could be a tough crowd because they often really grilled their speakers. Hearing this, I did a quick search on Twitter for "Vistage Speakers" and found five. Using the @ sign, I asked them if they had any recommendations. Within two minutes, I had a variety of responses like "Use statistics and case studies" and "Best of luck! Let us know how it goes." Folks I had never met before—one in China—were wishing me well.

This same experience has repeated itself in various areas. When I first got my dog, Snoopy, I had no idea what it was like to raise a puppy. I'd frequently turn to my Twitter followers and ask, "Do puppies eat peanuts?" or, "My puppy sleeps a lot! Is that normal?" I always get excellent answers.

Tom Morris, writer and philosopher, wrote an insightful article called "Twisdom: Twitter Wisdom" for the *Huffington Post* (www .HuffingtonPost.com, September 9, 2009). Morris writes:

> Twitter is not mainly about telling the world, or your forty-seven followers, what you had for lunch. And it's not just about Ashton and Oprah, or who can attract the most followers the quickest. It's about building a new form of community. It's about learning. It's about support, inspiration, and daily motivation. And it's also about fun. But the most important aspect of Twitter may be that, if you do things right, you begin to surround yourself with an incredible group of people eager to share their best questions and insights about life. They're all looking for new wisdom and hope. Twisdom is the result.
>
> There's collaborative thinking on Twitter at a level and in a form I've never seen before. Almost every day, and often many

times a day, a topic comes up that causes me, as a philosopher and simply a curious individual, to ponder a bit, and then share the results of that pondering in the 140 character increments, or "tweets" that Twitter allows. One comment will spark another, and before long, people of different ages and walks of life from around the world are engaged with me and each other in an extended conversation of brief bursts that add up to new realizations for everyone involved.

Multiple Twitter Accounts

Can you have multiple Twitter accounts? Yes. Should you have multiple accounts? It depends. Some people have an account for business twittering and another for personal twittering. I think this is a difficult balance to maintain because it is tough enough to get traction going for one Twitter account. However, it can be done. Dave Taylor (www.AskDaveTaylor.com) does a great job with his business account (www.twitter.com/FilmBuzz) and maintains a personal account as well. I have seen others successfully maintain business accounts, offering coupons, monetary deals, and so on. There are also service-oriented accounts that tweet current deals or respond to customer service issues. There are news services that tweet only headlines. You can choose what type of an account you want. Be careful, though: it needs to be something that people value or enjoy. Dave's business account is successful at least partially because film trivia and reviews are something that people enjoy more often than not.

Following and Unfollowing

We've discussed who you should follow, but can you unfollow someone who isn't providing value? Absolutely. If someone you follow doesn't add value to your life, feel free to stop following him or her. This is not an etiquette issue.

How do you get people to follow you? Try the following.

- Don't answer Twitter's question ("What are you doing?") literally. No one really cares about the fact that you just brushed your teeth or have to go pick up the kids from school, unless you can make it valuable. Avoid saying, "Going to pick up kids." Instead, say, "Picking up kids from school. I-35 and Beltline are jammed. Find another route." That's helpful!
- Leave out mundane details *unless* they add value. Avoid things like, "Loving this veggie burger." Use, "Loving this veggie burger at the new San Francisco joint on 45th and Lemon @VeggieTimeSF."
- Share valuable content. If you find a great site or useful tidbit, share. It's also okay to share content that you wrote yourself, as long as it's useful. My company gets 20 percent of our website traffic from Twitter using this method. Note: If you are sharing feedback on a place you've just visited, the latest article you've read, or someone's video link, see if you can find the creator's Twitter name and be sure to mention them in your tweet. This makes it much more likely that they will see your tweet and gives you a greater chance of being retweeted (further expanding your reach to a new group of followers).
- Ask genuine questions and welcome feedback. While writing this book, I often turned to my Twitter followers and asked what they would like to see addressed. Thoughtful questions can also lead to engaging discussions that can help you better understand others' perspectives and obtain feedback. This is key to building relationships.
- Put a button on your blog or website that invites people to follow you. One of the buttons we are most thankful for right now is Twitter's very own Follow button, a small widget that can be easily integrated onto a website. Your site's visitors can quickly click the small "Follow" button without leaving your site, and you've gained a follower on Twitter. Another thing you can do to promote your Twitter presence is designate a plot of your website real estate to a Twitter

feed. This is a widget that can greatly liven up your site and give your visitors some real-time updates straight from your mouth...uh, keyboard. The Twitter button can be found at https://dev.twitter.com/docs/follow-button.

- Make it a point to follow at least two new interesting people per day and send them a quick note commenting on how much value you've found reading their tweets. They may follow you back!

- Host a contest or giveaway. Many high-profile bloggers have done this. They ask people to follow them and retweet their contest message to enter the contest, so their name is spread quickly. This works if (1) you already have a good following (at least a few hundred), and (2) the giveaway is solid. You can also partner with industry-related bloggers or influencers who have Twitter accounts and have them host the contest for you. (You provide the prize, of course!)

- Don't ask people to help you get more followers to reach a certain number. It looks awful. It is okay to ask *if* you have a goal that isn't about your follower number. Avoid saying, "Please help me get to 500 followers. I am so close. Thanks." Instead, try, "I'd love to meet more people in the Detroit area. Can you recommend any?"

- When tweeting links, shorten them using a URL-shortening service. This way, you can fit more characters into a single tweet. Also, many URL-shortening services, like goog.gl, ow.ly, and bit.ly, allow you to track how many clicks a link receives. This is a great way to figure out what attracts folks to your website—and then do more of it!

Do the numbers matter? Yes. I wish I could say that they don't, but the number of people who follow you does matter. Why? The more people who follow you, the greater the reach you have. Today, when I ask a question or need feedback on an idea, I get 10 to 20 replies very quickly—and that's with 35,000 followers. So, yes, numbers matter.

Does this mean that you should obsess over the number of people following you? No. It's still better to focus on a smaller pool of people with whom you have connected rather than thousands with whom you haven't. You want to manage quality carefully as you increase quantity. As more and more people follow you, you can find tools that will help you categorize and organize the tweets. If you use TweetDeck, for example, you can organize your followers into categories. I have mine set up into two rows. The first contains all my followers, and the second is a list of colleagues and personal friends.

A Word on Auto-Following and Automated Direct Messaging

There are many applications out there that will allow you to auto-follow, meaning automatically following back those who follow you. There are also applications that let you do automated direct messaging, in which you send a canned direct message to all your followers. I don't recommend either technique.

When Twitter was new, automatically following people was a good way to give kudos (if you follow me, I will follow you back) and to grow your network. However, because Twitter has grown so rapidly, it has attracted its share of spammers. Unlike Facebook, which monitors and suspends accounts for even remotely suspicious activity, Twitter takes a more laissez-faire approach in governing. Spammers are notorious for following people who auto-follow and then unfollowing them. This skews their count so it looks like 10,000 people are following them and they are only following a handful. Can you think of any reason why 10,000 people would follow a spammer? Of course not. This is the whole point of their trick. They make it seem like they are legitimate by taking advantage of those who auto-follow.

Automated direct messaging is also a huge Twitter don't. There was a time when I believed automated messages could work when used properly, but because of Twitter's growth and users' misuse of the function by spammers, I recommend against it.

Using Twitter to Attract, Convert, and Transform

Twitter is one of those rare social networking sites where you can do all three! You can attract people to your website, convert followers into consumers and customers, and transform your past successes by sharing stories and case studies.

Posting links is a great way to attract people to your website. I once wrote a post called "10 Things to Do Immediately After a Networking Event" that included a link to our company blog. It led to 1,125 visits to our company blog when I tweeted it (and others retweeted it). That one article with a link attracted over a thousand people! Of that thousand, many chose to subscribe to the blog, becoming permanent consumers. Some will go on to convert into clients.

There are also times when we find people tweeting to search for something—such as web design, SEO, or social media help—in lieu of asking a friend or using a search engine. When we find such folks, we offer—without being pushy—to help them. It's even better when someone who is following us tells them, "Hey, The Marketing Zen Group does that kind of work well. Connect with @Shama." Often that turns them into an instant client for us!

Then, when we do the work, we share our results. For example, I might say, "Just launched a new website for Sal's Pizza! Check it out here: www.sals-pizza.com. That was a great project!" Or, we might share a case study or a story. This is difficult to do in 140 characters, but it can be accomplished with some practice. For example: "Client needed to reach a very targeted audience. Set up a Facebook page and targeted group XYZ. Got 800 clicks and a 20% increase in sales."

Getting Started on Twitter: The Power of Influencers

This content was originally shared as a post on The Marketing Zen Group blog, but we've decided to add it into the book because it details a strategy that can truly make or break your Twitter launch, and get you moving toward Twitter stardom. Now that we've covered how to set up a profile, it's time to make Twitter work for you.

The day you decide to get your blog/company/brand/self on Twitter is the same day you should commit to reaching out to at least ten people/companies/organizations multiple times in the coming weeks; let's call these people your "influencers."

Please note, when I say influencers I am referring to Twitter users who excel in the following:

- Valuable Content (their content is engaging, relevant, useful/unique)
- Appropriate Frequency (they tweet daily, with a good number of posts/day)
- High Quality Interaction (they are not spammers or RT-addicts)

If the users you discover have these three items nailed down, it is highly probable that they have been listed and followed by many others. It is important that you find a handful of influencers to interact with rather than just start sending out tweets to every other person you come across, because the right influencers are the people that can help you extend your reach, heighten your visibility, and ultimately gain Twitter followers for your blog/business/organization/self.

Your First Task: Write a List of Keywords

Write a list of keywords (to search for on Twitter), including industry occupations and common glossary terms, that would help direct you to:

- Twitter users in your industry (businesses/organizations/associations)
- Twitter users who write about your industry (media/industry journals and publications)
- Twitter users who are your competitors

Writing your list digitally is best so that you can copy/paste keywords into Twitter's search field when you're ready to discover your influencers.

Your Second Task: The Big Twitter Search-Off

- Search your top keywords, popular competitors, and industry associations.
- See who:
  a) they are following
  b) is mentioning them
  c) is following them
  d) is listing them
  e) is RT-ing them
  ...all in that order.
- Start clicking on the Twitter usernames you see, and look through their lists to find new and interesting people you'd like to follow.
- If you find a potential influencer, add them to your potential influencers list for any future marketing or PR efforts.

(See "Searching Twitter to Join Relevant Conversations" for more search tips.)

Your Third Task: Investigate

After you've compiled a list of Twitter users-of-interest, ask yourself the following questions:

- Is their content valuable to your audiences? (Is it engaging, relevant, useful/unique?)
- Was their last post yesterday? Are they tweeting three to eight posts throughout the day, every/almost every day, and including a mix of original content, RTs, and Mentions?
- Are their interactions (RTs and Mentions) relevant to your business/industry/audiences?

Extra Credit Task: Record the list of Twitter users you find, giving them grades. Here is a basic "Twitter Influencer Grade Report" format:

- Twitter Handle | Type of Product/Service/Business | Followers: # | Listed: #
- Twitter Profile Bio:
- URL:
- Tweet:
- Frequency:
- Level: Low – Med – High
- Score: 1 or 2
  1: Great content you would share with your audience; looks like they would be interested in sharing your content; influencer potential.
  2: Too many personal tweets and RTs and not enough original/valuable/relevant information or interaction with other users.

Your Fourth Task: Pick Your Top Ten Influencers and Go!

Analyze the grade report you developed during task 3. This report is something you can quickly scan and use to determine the first ten people you will try to develop a relationship with (through sharing valuable content, mutual RTing, and mentioning). Look at how you've ranked them and choose ten to start out with based on the areas most important to you. Note: It may be hard to keep up with more than ten when you're just getting started or if you are the lone social media resource for your company.

Once you have your ten, make your presence known and begin building those relationships!

- Make sure that your feed is fairly developed when you start reaching out to your influencers; i.e., do not have three tweets on your profile with promotional messaging and zero original tweets. Start out with a welcome tweet with a quick blurb of the purpose of your Twitter profile. Then RT a few relevant articles and craft a few posts related to your activity as a blogger/company/interest (something your potential followers will connect with and find value in).

- RT their original content. Mention them and give your opinion and/or ask questions about their statements in a piece of content they've produced. They will likely reply to you by mentioning your name (if your note sounds genuine and is not attacking them). If your tweet is as valuable/innovative/smart/relevant to the influencer's audience as it should be, the influencer's audience may look into following you, too.
- Thank them for sharing a valuable tip. Write a custom message for your audience on why it is a good link and mention the influencer at the end of it, so they are alerted of your "review." They will likely RT your tweet because of its positive testimony.

It is always important—no matter where you are sharing/posting/tweeting content—to ask yourself, how would I respond to this messaging? If you critique your message with this question in mind and find yourself feeling negatively about it, it is time to try again. Remember, you are projecting information to humans who can tell trash from treasure within an instant.

Searching Twitter to Join Relevant Conversations

Knowing how to search on Twitter is crucial because that is how you know which conversations to join! Practicing savvy searching skills on Twitter is like practicing good listening skills in a face-to-face conversation. If you don't search, you won't know who is looking for you—and, perhaps more importantly, who might have a complaint or concern. Complaints and concerns are best addressed publicly so others can see that you are a company that cares and is tuned in. Many big companies such as Comcast, Dell, and JetBlue use Twitter to offer customer service. They search for mentions of their name and engage those users in a useful conversation.

You can search Twitter conversations directly from your Twitter home page. What should you search for? Your company name, your personal name, and any industry-related terms. Also, be sure to search for phrases related to the service or product you offer. For example, if you are a web designer, you should search for "need website." This is one of the beautiful things about Twitter. People *often* search for what they need in a very public manner. It is not uncommon to see people asking for referrals and recommendations. *And* it is okay to offer up your product or company in a nonintrusive manner. Recently, I was searching for some project-management software, and I asked for recommendations. Shortly afterward, two owners of project-management software companies asked whether I had seen their site and if I would like a demo. This is a great example of selling made simple. Best of all, because I was looking for this information, I was grateful to hear from them.

Here are three stories on how I have leveraged Twitter to further my own business:

1. **Snagged a speaking engagement**: I follow the founder of a very prestigious blogging conference. I had just submitted my speaking proposal through his website when I sent him a public message giving him a heads-up on the proposed topic. No sooner had I sent out that tweet than a well-known blogger retweeted the message and added something along the lines of "you would be missing out if she didn't present." Almost immediately, I got a direct message from the founder saying he liked the topic and that I was in. It all happened within seconds! Don't underestimate the power of Twitter. Since then, people have often noticed my speaking topics when I tweet and asked me to speak at their events.

2. **Found direct clients**: We get at least two leads a week from Twitter. Someone inevitably sees a tweet about a website we just finished, or a ranking we achieved for a client, and wants to know what we can do for him or her. That is social media at its best, because you are attracting new clients by transforming your old successes into stories—or, in this case, tweets!

3. **Established expertise**: We once had a client who hired us solely by looking at my tweets. He said they were proof that we knew online marketing; our tips on Twitter convinced him. Establishing my expertise has led to multiple speaking opportunities, more clients, and articles in various publications. It has also led to some great joint venture relationships. Colleagues who do complementary work will often see what we do and refer their clients to us. It is a win-win situation for all.

Some Useful Tools for Twitter Search

Get help from Twitter:
- Twitter's Guide to Search: bit.ly/SearchTW
- Twitter's Advanced Search: twitter.com/#!/search-advanced

Find relevant Twitter users faster:
- Twellow.com
- FollowerWonk.com

Find relevant Twitter lists (following uber-relevant users) faster:
- Listorious.com

Find local Twitter users with:
- TwitterLocal.net
- Twellow.com/twellowhood
- LocalTweeps.com

Twitter Applications

Because Twitter continues to grow at such a fast pace, applications to bolster it are being created on a daily basis. Here are a few of my favorites:

- Gremln (www.gremln.com): Gremln allows you to schedule your tweets, create groups, manage multiple users, and monitor your brand.
- TweetDeck (www.TweetDeck.com): TweetDeck allows you to manage Twitter on your desktop. It shows you the tweets of people you're following, replies, and direct messages in three clean columns. No clicking back and forth necessary!
- SocialOomph (www.SocialOomph.com): SocialOomph allows you to release tweets in the future. Going on a vacation but found some good content to share? You can use this application to write tweets ahead of time to post automatically while you're gone.

- HootSuite (HootSuite.com): HootSuite allows you to track multiple accounts and supports multiple users. It also lets you track statistics such as how many people clicked on your last link.
- TwitPic (www.TwitPic.com): TwitPic allows you to share pictures on Twitter. It's very easy to use! However, due to Twitter's latest image integration project, Galleries, TwitPic's future is a little uncertain.
- Twitterfeed (Twitterfeed.com): Twitterfeed is a service that feeds your blog to Twitter. Use it in moderation! You don't want your Twitter stream to be full of your own posts.

Twitter on Your Phone?

There are a number of applications that allow you to tweet using your phone, as well. Here are a few:

- Twitterific (Twitterrific.com): Twitterific is a tried-and-true application for the iPhone.
- ÜberTwitter (www.UberTwitter.com): ÜberTwitter is a good tool for using Twitter on your BlackBerry.
- Twitter Mobile (m.twitter.com): Twitter Mobile is Twitter's own mobile site.
- TweetDeck: TweetDeck for mobile is basically as good as the desktop version.

Twitter Do's and Don'ts

DO:
- ✓ Use your tweets strategically. Know what you are trying to accomplish with your tweet.
- ✓ Follow people you admire, even if they don't follow you back.
- ✓ Be on the lookout for valuable content to share with your followers.
- ✓ Treat your followers with respect. There are lots of viewpoints on Twitter, and without nonverbal cues, it's easy to offend people. Use sarcasm with care.

- ✓ Respond to direct messages and @ replies.
- ✓ Create a community of colleagues.
- ✓ Ask genuine questions—you'll get good answers!
- ✓ Retweet when someone shares something valuable.
- ✓ Share relevant pictures and videos.
- ✓ Work on attracting people to your site (using real value, not pushy links).
- ✓ Share mini–case studies about your successes.
- ✓ Learn to tell stories in 140 characters.
- ✓ Track how many people click on your tweeted links, RT your content, and follow people who mention and RT you.

DON'T:

- ☒ Try to force anyone to follow you. I have seen people get angry because someone won't follow them back. You can only decide who to follow—not who follows you.
- ☒ Ask someone why they unfollowed you. Respect their decision.
- ☒ Mass-follow people. (Really *look* at who you want to follow. This is your chance to create your own human search engine.)
- ☒ Post links only to *your* website. (No one likes someone who constantly self-promotes.)
- ☒ Twitter when sleepy or inebriated.
- ☒ Ask followers to help you reach a certain number of followers.
- ☒ Promote something you haven't tried yourself, just to make a few bucks.
- ☒ Tweet something you wouldn't want someone to find. (Tweets are indexed by Google and can come up in people's search results.)

How to Be Proactive on Twitter

The following tips will help you use Twitter proactively.

- **Get instant market feedback.** When I asked my followers on Twitter which they would prefer—an e-book or a whole course on social media marketing—I immediately got answers and rationales. Twitter is a *great* way to test out your ideas before taking them any further. You do need to have a few hundred followers for this to be a successful test.
- **Show your followers respect.** There are companies out there who will pay you to tweet ads in the form of links. The bigger your follower base, the more you get paid. This is an awful way to monetize on Twitter. I have seen the backlash firsthand when I tested a service called Magpie. It doesn't matter if you actually have used the products you are advertising; people see it as an intrusion. Don't advertise outside products using Twitter.

- **Let people sample your style and work.** If blogs and websites are novels, tweets are short stories. Twitter is a great way to allow people to taste a sample of your work. Tweet tips related to your industry, and let your personality shine through. If you are witty, be witty. If you are known for your warm nature, show that to the world!
- **Generate quality traffic.** You can generate some quality traffic from Twitter because followers have already sampled your work or style. They may even feel like they already know you! The best traffic is generated when you share a content link from your website and people retweet it.
- **Build trust.** Social media is very much about transparency. The lines between personal and professional are blurred. Twitter is your chance to build trust with influencers and future clients and customers just by being yourself! We trust people with whom we come into contact more than we trust strangers.
- **Generate content.** Twitter is the #1 spot to find guest bloggers and interviewees. Have a blog? A podcast? Want to interview someone? Twitter is a great way to reach out to him or her!
- **Generate ideas.** If you just "listen in" on Twitter, you can see immediately that it is a marketplace buzzing with ideas. People are asking questions (that you can potentially provide answers to) and sharing thoughts. There are many movers and shakers on Twitter!
- **Get online PR.** As noted previously, bloggers hang out on Twitter a lot. And you know what bloggers have? Communities of followers. Twitter is a great way to make friends with bloggers and reporters. Be genuine. They need stories as much as you need the press.
- **Find people to hire.** There are some very talented folks on Twitter. Whenever we are hiring, we look there first by sending out a tweet to let our followers know we are hiring, and by searching specific phrases such as "web developer + Dallas." We have hired two interns we found on Twitter.

- **Manage your reputation.** Every day I see at least three people or companies being talked about that are not on Twitter and probably don't have a clue as to what is being said about them. Don't be like them. Twitter is a great way to see what people have to say about your service and product. You can also use Twitter as a customer service tool, answering questions and taking queries live. Already give great customer service? Perfect! Use Twitter to make it transparent.
- **Send out your newsletter.** Many newsletter services these days will send out a link to your newsletter through your Twitter account when they send out your newsletter via email. iContact (www.icontact.com), AWeber (www.AWeber .com), MailChimp (www.MailChimp.com), and Constant Contact (www.constantcontact.com) all have this feature.

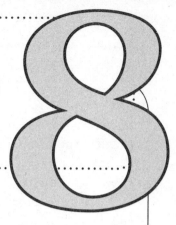

LinkedIn

The Social Media Platform for Professionals

Why Bother with LinkedIn?

- It has more than 38 million registered members from over 200 countries.
- It's a network geared toward professionals looking to network—the members are there to talk shop!
- It is excellent for online visibility.
- It's a great way to showcase expertise.
- It serves as the ultimate online Rolodex.
- Via LinkedIn Pulse, it's an effective publishing platform for thought leadership industry articles as part of your content marketing strategy.

LinkedIn is like a buttoned-down office event. If Facebook is happy hour, LinkedIn is all business, in a suit and tie. It's especially useful to those in the business-to-business (B2B) sphere because it allows you to connect to specific decision-makers better than any other.

LinkedIn Basics

LinkedIn is a great way to connect with former bosses, colleagues, and clients. Chances are, they are there!

LinkedIn offers both free and paid accounts. A paid account allows you to send InMails (email messages within LinkedIn) to those who are accepting them. This is a good way to reach people who may not currently be in your network. A paid account is not necessary, however, to make the most of LinkedIn.

LinkedIn allows you to give and receive professional recommendations, and you can choose to feature these on your profile. This is an excellent feature to showcase your aptitude and talent. Much of LinkedIn is about creating an interactive résumé for yourself.

Everything you need to know about LinkedIn can be divided into four segments: your profile, managing contacts, Pulse, and groups.

LinkedIn is really your résumé on steroids. The site has a number of advanced applications that allow you to promote your products, services, events, businesses, and brand, and drive targeted traffic to your websites. It also ranks extremely high in Google's search engine, which gives you another platform to promote your name when someone searches for you.

If you want to bring your business or brand to the next level, then it is critical to take action and start optimizing LinkedIn to achieve your goals.

Lewis Howes,
coauthor of LinkedWorking

Your LinkedIn Profile

Think of your LinkedIn profile as an interactive online résumé. Your colleagues, prospects, and vendors can all see your professional life in a nutshell. Here is a screenshot of the first part of my profile:

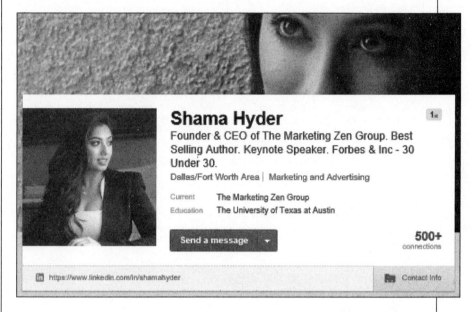

Use the following tips to create the best LinkedIn profile for yourself.

- Use a good headshot, ideally one that frames your full face and shows you smiling! (You can use the same one across all social media sites.)
- When you receive recommendations from colleagues and clients, showcase them on your profile. When someone posts a recommendation, you will get a message asking you to accept.
- Your summary is key. Write it to be read. Use adjectives, and make it pack a punch. It's okay if you have to rewrite it a few times. It can (and should) be a work in progress. Here is a screenshot of my current summary:

Summary

Known as the "Zen Master of Marketing" by Entrepreneur Magazine and the "Millennial Master of the Universe" by Fast Company, Shama Hyder is a visionary strategist for the digital age.

She is the bestselling author of the Zen of Social Media Marketing and an acclaimed international keynote speaker who has been invited to share the speaking stage with the world's top leaders, including President Obama and the Dalai Lama.

A trusted media expert and sought-after TV personality, Shama has frequently appeared on Fox Business, CBS, CW33 and Fox News. As a thought leader, she's been featured in many major publications, including The New York Times, The Wall Street Journal, Business Week, Huffington Post, Entrepreneur, Inc Magazine and Forbes.

As the CEO of the award-winning Marketing Zen Group, she's led the organization through explosive growth, averaging 400% growth annually since its start in 2009. Under her leadership, the company has grown to include a team of 30 and clients that range from publicly held, Fortune 500 companies to privately held small businesses and non-profit organizations across the globe. As a result of her success, Shama has been the recipient of the prestigious Technology Titan Emerging Company CEO award. She was also named one of the "Top 25 Entrepreneurs under 25" by Business Week in 2009 and one of the "Top 30 under 30" Entrepreneurs in America in 2013.
In addition, Shama has been honored at the White House and the United Nations as one of the top 100 young entrepreneurs in North America.

Beyond her roles as a media personality, international speaker, and CEO, she also serves as a mentor to the next generation of entrepreneurs. She is passionate about empowering youth and works closely with the Young Entrepreneur Council in fostering youth entrepreneurship around the world.

She was recently named to the Forbes 30 Under 30 list of Movers and Shakers for 2015.

Inc. | Inc. Magazine Interviews

In the C-Suite: Inc Live Chat with Shama Hyder

• In your summary, use keywords that make it easy for other people to search for you. Include industry terms as well as layman's terms. For example, for the longest time, the airline industry thought everyone was searching for "low airfare," only to discover that most were looking for "cheap tickets."

• Remember to check your spelling. This is a professional networking site, and the rules (though unwritten) are a bit more stringent. Whereas someone may forgive a spelling slipup on

Twitter or Facebook, on LinkedIn misspelling a word is comparable to making a spelling error on your résumé.

- The Skills area directly beneath your summary allows you to "tag" yourself appropriately. Think about how others may categorize you or search for you. What keywords would you want someone to use to find you? Also, what specifically do you specialize in? You will notice that in my Skills section I include "online marketing" (which is very broad so people can find me under that category) and also "social media marketing" (which is a specialty). A bonus with this section: Other LinkedIn users can also click or "endorse" you for specific skills.

- LinkedIn allows you to make your profile public. If you are planning to use LinkedIn as a marketing tool, by all means make it public. This allows search engines to find you as well, making keyword usage even more important.

Managing Contacts

Who should you connect with on LinkedIn?

- Past and current bosses: It's especially important to add those with whom you have a good relationship; they are great folks to get recommendations from.
- Your clients and customers: If you have a huge list of customers, only add those with whom you have connected personally via email or phone. In other words, add only those who would recognize your name!
- Industry contacts such as vendors, distributors, and resellers: Essentially, add all business contacts.
- Bloggers who cover your industry or might cover your product: Not all bloggers will be open to connecting on LinkedIn, but some will.

Pulse

Pulse is a daily news app that is personalized for each user. Any LinkedIn user can add a post to Pulse, making it an excellent publishing platform to add to your content marketing strategy.

What type of content should you post to Pulse? First, stay away from anything "salesy" or promotional. What you do want to post are articles that demonstrate your thought leadership and expertise in your business marketplace or industry.

Some ideas for Pulse topics include:

- Opinion pieces on major industry news, such as a merger or acquisition.

- Forward-thinking articles that offer insight into where you believe your business space is heading.
- General knowledge pieces where you break down complex topics and provide tips, tactics, or strategies that position you as a subject matter expert.

You can use your company for case study examples, but you want to stay away from promoting your brand, products, or services.

LinkedIn Groups

LinkedIn groups are similar to Facebook groups. They're a great way to find people with similar interests. Once you have joined a group, it will appear near the bottom of your profile page on your left-side navigation bar under "Groups." Here are some ways LinkedIn groups can be useful:

- **They let you send InMail to members without having to upgrade.** This feature itself makes LinkedIn groups useful. If you try to message someone who isn't connected to you, LinkedIn will ask you to upgrade. Join a group that that person is a member of, and you can send him or her a message without upgrading. Again, this works best if you have a genuine interest in the group and aren't using this feature as a spam mechanism.
- **They're a great way to communicate with your group or organization online.** Look under the "Discussions" tab on your group page to view current discussions or start your own.
- **Those searching for you can find you more easily.** If someone is searching for a speaker, he or she is likely to find you more easily if you are already part of a LinkedIn speaker's group.

To find groups to join, look through LinkedIn's group directory at https://www.linkedin.com/directory/groups. In certain groups, your membership may have to be reviewed by a group manager before you are accepted. For instance, college- or company-related groups may require an email address associated with the college or company. If you have questions about a group, you can send a message to the owner listed on the group information page.

LinkedIn Do's and Don'ts

For the ultimate do's and don'ts on LinkedIn, I reached out to Jason Alba (CEO of JibberJobber and author of *I'm on LinkedIn— Now What???*), Mike O'Neil (CEO of Integrated Alliances), and Viveka von Rosen (Always Extraordinary). I asked all three LinkedIn experts to provide me with unique do's and don'ts that are often overlooked. The first four tips in the first list and the first five tips in the second were provided by Jason; the rest were provided by Mike and Viveka.

DO:
- ✓ **Flesh out your profile.** Too many profiles are sparse, with little information. Not only does this decrease your chances of being found when someone is searching for talent, but when someone does find your profile, he or she doesn't have much to go on.
- ✓ **Join groups.** When you join groups, you have extra privileges with group members that you would only have if you

were first-degree contacts. This is also a great way to find people who share like interests without having to find them in search results.

✓ **Use the advanced search.** This is a very powerful part of LinkedIn and can help you find contacts you should get in touch with or add to your network. Go beyond the basic search and explore the power of the advanced search.

✓ **Export your contacts.** I recommend you export your contact list to create a backup, and also take it a step further: import them into a CRM (customer relationship management) tool. That way you can manage the relationships with more detail without being subject to LinkedIn's restrictions.

✓ **Treat your LinkedIn profile like a website.** Make sure it is well-formatted, clean, and, most importantly, of interest to others. Ask friends to read it, and ask them to be very critical in their assessments. This should not be an "attaboy" moment.

✓ **Populate your LinkedIn profile with keywords.** The

keywords should reflect your background, your industry, and the industries of your *clients* to make it easier for potential clients to find you. Be sure to include the variants of the words (teach, teacher, taught, teaching), the synonyms of those words (speaker, educator), and the variants of *those* words (speaking, education).

✓ **Make your page visually interesting.** Look into using special symbols (✈ ◊ ■ ↔ ◆) to break up your text and add emphasis to key elements.

DON'T:

☒ **Spam.** Don't come to LinkedIn hoping to hawk your wares. This is a place to network, and business happens here, but people want to focus on relationships, not listen to your next cool pitch. Make sure you are authentic and care about them before you start talking too much about your company or product.

☒ **Forget who might see your profile.** Getting too casual or too serious, or not being compelling enough, might cost you in business or opportunities. Have your profile ready for your target audience, and when they find it, you'll have the credibility you need.

☒ **Misunderstand the concept of connections.** Will you connect with everyone? What about your competition? Or will you connect with only people you have met in person? Everyone has a different connection strategy appropriate to him or her. You need to figure out your own connection strategy.

☒ **Send canned invitations.** When you invite someone, go into the invitation message and customize it. Let him or her know who you are and why you want to connect.

☒ **Preach.** I get invitations on LinkedIn telling me all the virtues of LinkedIn. When I see these invitations, I know the senders have not read my profile, and I assume they are just adding me to increase their numbers (as opposed to wanting to develop a relationship with me).

☒ Use anything in your name field that doesn't belong as part of your name. For example, don't use "Paul A. (Pablo_paul@yahoo.com), PABLO A." when you can use "Pablo Paul," or LinkedIn users will not be able to find you when searching for you by name. This is also a violation of the LinkedIn User Agreement, and you don't want to lose your account.

☒ Put anything in the picture area but a headshot picture of yourself. No group pictures, no kids, no spouse, no logo. A professional photo is not required—just use a simple headshot picture from any standard digital camera. LinkedIn will help you crop it to the required 85 × 85 pixels.

☒ Include only recent jobs, as you may be tempted to do. Put in all of your work history, back to college days. This gives you more inroads to create more relationships with others.

☒ Use paragraphs longer than five lines as they appear in the View My Profile section. Break up paragraphs with six or more lines into multiple paragraphs.

AHA! Zen Moment

How should you ACT on LinkedIn?

Attract: Create a compelling profile. Use LinkedIn groups to connect with others who might be good referral sources or potential joint venture partners.

Convert: Use the Pulse feature to get strangers to consume your content and perhaps even turn into clients!

Transform: Get recommendations from your contacts on LinkedIn. This is a great way to showcase your expertise! 🧘

How to Be Proactive on LinkedIn

The following tips will help you use LinkedIn proactively.

- **Gain more visibility.** By adding connections, you further the likelihood that someone will find you when they need you. Write a compelling profile, and keep your contact database updated with your professional contacts.
- **Increase your rank with search engines.** LinkedIn allows you the option of making your profile public, which will allow search engines to index it. This is a very smart move, because LinkedIn is ranked very highly by search engines. When you create a public profile, select "Full View." Instead of using the default URL LinkedIn provides, customize your public profile's URL to include your actual name.
- **Get business advice.** LinkedIn Groups are a great way to get advice and find answers to your most pressing questions. This is an especially useful tool if you are a business-to-business company.
- **Conduct market research.** Not sure what your potential clients or customers feel their greatest need is? Just ask. Need to test out the market with a new idea? Ask for feedback. LinkedIn Groups make it easy.

The Many Flavors of Social Media

EVER HEARD THE SAYING, *Social media never sleeps*? There's a reason why social media shares an adage with none other than the Big Apple—both are places of constant activity, especially the continuous rise and fall of new trends.

Sure, some social media platforms make the big time and establish themselves as power players for the long haul (Facebook, Twitter, and LinkedIn, I'm looking at you!). But plenty of others arrive on the scene, enjoy a season of popularity, and then slowly fizzle out (remember Friendster and MySpace?).

So how's a marketer to know which of the new platforms popping up every day they should spend time building a presence on, and which they should ignore?

Unfortunately, there's no simple formula to determine whether a new platform will take off, or whether a popular platform will remain popular long term.

Take Google+, for example. With so much support from parent Google thrown behind it, this was a channel that seemed destined for greatness from the very start! Google all but required its massive user base to create Google+ accounts, making it a prerequisite for logging into Google properties such as YouTube. Their search algorithm was changed to boost the rankings of content shared via Google+ posts. Even the unique structure of Google+, with its organization into Circles, seemed like a winning choice for a social media channel.

But, alas, it was not to be. While it did enjoy temporary, modest success when it first launched, Google+ quickly fell out of favor with users. Marketers who had hoped to take advantage of the channel for audience engagement were mostly disappointed in that regard, although they were able to harness the power of its SEO benefits. Today, aside from occasionally posting to the platform to help their search engine rankings, marketers have pretty much given up on Google+.

Where Google+ failed, however, others are succeeding. There are plenty of newer social media platforms attracting the attention of consumers and marketers alike. The key to choosing the right ones? A careful consideration of how each fits into your overall marketing strategy.

By looking into the demographics of each new platform, along with the behavior of its users, you can determine whether it's a place where your time and effort will be well spent, reaching your target audience in a way that will attract, convert, and transform—or whether you're better off looking elsewhere.

To help you get started, let's take a look at some of the strongest secondary players in social media today: the more established Instagram, Pinterest, and Snapchat, along with newer up-and-comers Imgur and LINE.

Instagram

Why Bother with Instagram?

- It has 400 million monthly active users and is still growing.
- It's split almost evenly between male and female users.

- It reaches 34 percent of the total U.S. digital population.
- It's used by 55 percent of online adults aged 18 to 29.
- It has a global audience: 70 percent of its users are outside the United States.

Instagram is definitely where the cool kids hang out online. A photo- and video-sharing platform, it's become the place to show off artsy photos of your trendy restaurant meals and inspiring pictures of your morning yoga routine. More focused on images than text, Instagram brings out the photographer in its users, who are quick to appreciate great shots shared by anyone—even businesses—as long as the marketing isn't too blatant. This platform can be a gold mine for B2C companies looking to engage with their audience—especially those with a strong visual element to their brand.

Instagram Basics

Instagram is sort of like Twitter for images, but it's owned by a different social media giant: Facebook acquired Instagram back in 2012. Users take a photo or video, choose a "filter" to apply to make the shot look even better, and then post it with a comment and even hashtags, if desired. Followers can then like and comment on that post.

However, unlike Twitter and Facebook, Instagram is much more about giving your audience glimpses into your company culture and strategic product placement in gorgeous shots than it is about sharing more obvious marketing-related content.

Here's how to get started:

1. The first step in marketing on Instagram is to **fill out your bio.** This includes making sure you have links to all your other social media pages to enable interested consumers to connect with you in other ways.
2. Next, **think strategically** about the kinds of photos you want to share. What kind of company image do you want to

convey? How will you get your message across? How will your photos drive engagement and traffic to your website?

3. When you start taking photos, **pay attention to picture quality.** Yes, Instagram is a place to share snapshots taken with your phone's camera. But that doesn't mean they can be poor quality. Don't share shots that are confusing or blurry. Make sure they're worthy of representing your company. And don't forget to play around with the different filters that are built into the Instagram interface. You can even use a different photo-editing app to get the look you want before importing the image into Instagram.

4. Because Instagram can be a "fun" social media platform that encourages posting and sharing, be careful and **don't go overboard.** Posting pictures regularly is great—but don't completely overwhelm your followers' feeds. A good way to determine how often to post is to do a little recon work: check out how often your competitors are posting, and then imitate that frequency.

5. Make sure you **don't forget the hashtags.** Just as with other social media platforms, hashtags are great marketing tools to help consumers find you, and very much a part of the Instagram user experience. Tap into popular hashtags, or even create your own.

6. If you are putting effort into marketing on Instagram and you have an engaged audience, don't forget to **respond to comments.** Just as with any other social media channel, people want and expect businesses to respond to their comments in a timely manner, even if it's just to say thanks. Make sure you are checking comments regularly, and take the time to continue the conversations you've inspired.

7. Finally, **share your Instagram pictures on other platforms.** Don't confine those great shots to one social media channel! Let your followers on other sites see what they're missing out on, so they'll be prompted to connect with you on

Instagram as well. The more touch points you have with your customers, the better!

Instagram Do's and Don'ts

DO:

- ✓ Use Instagram to tell a story with a series of images. You could show different people at the same event, or pictures that show each stage of setup for an event, for example. Be creative!
- ✓ Center images around the lifestyle that fits your brand image. If you're a hardworking, all-American company, try shots of cowboys and Americana. Sell luxury items? Share images of exotic beaches and five-star hotel lobbies.
- ✓ Creatively showcase your products. For example, find humorous new uses for one of your products, and share images of people trying them out. Or give tantalizing sneak previews of new products to come.
- ✓ Feature your customers. What better way is there to get people to engage than to post pictures of them?
- ✓ Hold contests. This is a great way to raise enthusiasm levels and get followers more involved with your brand. Be sure to check out the Promotion Guidelines in the Instagram Help Center first, to familiarize yourself with the rules.

DON'T:

- ☒ Post picture after picture of your products on Instagram. Trying to use Instagram to sell will only annoy your followers.
- ☒ Be afraid to share informal, behind-the-scenes photos or goofy shots. Instagram is all about creating a uniquely authentic relationship with your audience.
- ☒ Forget to experiment to see which types of photos get the most engagement. Do filters help, or hurt? Are gorgeous views or shots of people more popular? Find out what works for your audience.

How Should You ACT on Instagram?

Attract: Use hashtags to make it easy for people to stumble across your posts when searching for images like yours. Post photos that are beautiful or fun to increase followers.

Convert: Although it's not as direct a path as using other social media channels, building a strong relationship with your audience on Instagram will lead them to your website eventually. Be sure to engage authentically with them to build that connection with your brand.

Transform: This is where Instagram shines. Happy customers will often share photos of themselves with a favorite product; find brand advocates and inspire them to help you get your message out. 🧘

Pinterest

Why Bother with Pinterest?

- It has 100 million users …
- … of which 85 percent are female!
- It's used by 42 percent of U.S. adult women.
- Forty-five percent of its users are outside the United States.
- Sixty-seven percent of its users are under age 40.

Pinterest is Instagram's dressier, slightly older sister. Where Instagram loves artsy snapshots of coffee cups next to open books, Pinterest prefers professional-looking photographs of perfectly executed crafts. Where you might see a picture of bare feet and a twirling skirt in a field on Instagram, you'll find that same skirt on a model on the runway on Pinterest. As with Instagram, Pinterest is all about the image, but in a very different way. While

Instagram photos are snapshots of life, Pinterest images are formal photographs of things you like—or want. B2C companies can take advantage of Pinterest users' passion for beauty and perfection by creating gorgeous pinboards that showcase their products and the lifestyle to which they relate.

Pinterest Basics

Pinterest is very different from any other social media platform out there because of the unique way users interact with its content. Users create virtual pinboards, onto which they can pin images. When other users follow these pinboards, they see any new pins added. Re-pinning someone else's photo is a way to let them know you liked it, as well as share it with your own followers. And, of course, the standard options to like and comment on others' pins are also available.

Unlike Instagram users, Pinterest users are up for a little more obvious marketing, so promoting sales or pinning product pictures is perfectly fine here. Just be careful to balance those pins out with an approximately equal number of lifestyle-related pins, such as shots of exotic beaches to promote a swimsuit company or beautiful wedding pictures for an engagement ring store, to give your audience a reason to follow you.

Here's how to get started:

1. **Take the time to set up your Pinterest profile.** Match your branding to every other platform where you have a presence, and make sure you include links to your site for customers looking to learn more.
2. **Before you even take a single picture of your products, determine who your Pinterest audience is.** Who are you trying to attract with your images? Who is it you want to inspire to share your images with their own followers? As with any kind of social media marketing, you want to create a connection and build a relationship. So it's vital to have a clear understanding of who you're trying to connect with.

3. **Plan your boards strategically.** Don't create boards based simply on your store's different categories of products. Instead, create boards that are aimed at those ideal customers you just identified—boards that will show those potential customers that you get them, that you are like them, and that you offer things that will fill a gap in their lives. Use your board to tell an appealing story about how your products can improve their lives, rather than simply as a list.

4. **Be honest with yourself about your company's photography chops.** If someone on your team is a pro at getting the perfect shot, then by all means, take your own pictures. But if you're less than confident about your company's camera skills, don't hesitate to hire a good photographer.

5. **Decide on a different image for every single page, product, or important piece of content to which you want to draw attention.** You can use Pinterest to promote different pages of your website, different products or services you offer, and different content you want to share. But each individual pin needs to have its own distinctive, attractive image, or it won't be effective. You just can't get away with using your company logo over and over again for every single page of content you share, or using a clichéd graphic for a service you provide. Captions and blurbs will not sway people on Pinterest—the image is all that counts.

6. **Add a Pinterest icon to your site, and add Pinterest share tabs to every single image on your site.** Let people know you're on Pinterest, and make it easy for them to share your pictures there.

Once you've got your audience determined, your boards planned out, great images chosen, and convenient ways in place for customers to spread the word, you'll be able to jump into Pinterest and take off running.

Pinterest Do's and Don'ts

DO:

- ✓ Make separate boards to organize pins by theme. Often, those new to the site forget about this very basic function, and instead pin all of their photos to the same board.
- ✓ Crowdsource. Pinterest allows for pinboards with multiple contributors, so brands can create boards that invite audience participation. Crowdsourcing can also take the form of asking customers to pin photos to your board of themselves using your product in creative ways.
- ✓ Familiarize yourself with the Pinterest Acceptable Use Policy before launching any form of Pinterest marketing strategy—it draws a very precise line between marketing activities and spamming. For example, asking people to comment and telling people to vote with pins or likes are strictly against the rules.
- ✓ Re-pin, comment, and like. Don't make your Pinterest communication a one-way street—interact with people, even if they haven't initiated it!
- ✓ Use secret boards! Nothing gives customers more of a thrill than being invited to something secret. Create a secret board only for customers who have purchased a certain dollar amount of products or who have signed up for your loyalty program, and share images and content that are for their eyes only.

DON'T:

- ☒ Forget who you're targeting. Most social media sites aren't this heavily skewed to one gender, which means you'll probably need to adjust your marketing messaging to focus on women (unless you're already targeting that particular demographic).
- ☒ Get too pin-happy. Your Pinterest followers don't want to deal with the clutter you create when you pin photos all

day long. Pin in such a way that you won't completely overwhelm people into unfollowing your boards.

How Should You ACT on Pinterest?

Attract: Place Pinterest share tabs on every image on your site, so it's easy for people to share them. On Pinterest, reach out to your audience by re-pinning their pins, and they'll reciprocate, sharing your pins with their own followings.

Convert: Pinning images of products in seasonal settings is a great way to inspire people to buy. Make sure each of your images links back to the appropriate page on your website where they can easily make that purchase.

Transform: Pinterest is all about sharing images with others, so it's easy to gain real traction when your audience starts sharing your pins. 🧘

Snapchat

Why Bother with Snapchat?

- It boasts 100 million daily active users.
- It claims 4 billion daily video views.
- Seventy-one percent of its users are under age 34.
- Forty-five percent of its users are between ages 18 and 24.
- Seventy percent of its users are female.

Snapchat is an absolute gold mine for marketers looking to reach a Millennial audience: this mobile platform is wildly popular among that demographic, due in no small part to its unique, "self-destructing" posts, called snaps. Also heavily image-centric, Snapchat can be most effectively harnessed by B2C companies searching for a way to look trendy and hip. But marketing through

Snapchat is so tricky that publishing brands such as CNN, National Geographic, and Daily Mail all have dedicated Snapchat staff within their social media teams who specialize in the platform.

Snapchat Basics

Snapchat users send pictures or videos and set them to disappear after one to ten seconds. Snaps are shareable in real time with users' friends, and users also have the option to save snaps to their phone's photo gallery. Users can also add photos and videos of their own to their "Snapchat Story," where they can be viewed by their followers or the general public for twenty-four hours.

Although content on the platform is fleeting, the value comes in having the full attention of the Snapchat user when a snap is received, since users know they only have a limited time to view each one. One tactic that can be successful is marketing a limited-time discount, or an offer that includes an element of urgency that matches the time-sensitive Snapchat experience.

Here's how to get started:

1. **Download the app, and set up your Snapchat business account.** Choose your username wisely, because Snapchat has no user profile pages like other social media platforms do. Your username is the only way your audience will be able to tell who you are!

2. **Change your settings to allow "everyone" to view your Snapchat Story.** This way, when you post images or videos to your Story, they'll be public and findable through a search by anyone for twenty-four hours.

3. **Start sending snaps!** Take a picture or a video, and then send it to friends on your list, or directly to your Story. Be sure to play around with the available captions, emojis, drawings, and filters.

Snapchat Do's and Don'ts

DO:

✓ Offer sneak previews of new products. Snapchat is the

perfect platform to give a fleeting glimpse and leave consumers excited and wanting more.

✓ Go behind the scenes and take advantage of spur-of-the-moment events to give Snapchat users a sense of being an insider with your brand.

✓ Experiment with offers and rewards. Because posts are so ephemeral, the expiration date of the offer is built into the platform—an offer might expire when the snap does, for example, because the link disappears along with it.

DON'T:

☒ Use video without a solid strategy in place. Snapchat forces you to get your point across very quickly—in ten seconds or less—and research has found most Snapchatters only watch the first two or three seconds of video unless it's extremely engaging.

☒ Disregard paid advertising. Snapchat has a roster of publishers who have "Discover" channels on Snapchat, and it's possible to advertise on those channels to reach the Snapchat audience of specific publishing brands such as Vice, BuzzFeed, and ESPN.

——— AHA! Zen Moment ———

How Should You ACT on Snapchat?

Attract: Snapchat's paid ads may be the most efficient way to get you started by reaching large numbers of users.

Convert: The fleeting nature of snaps makes them perfect for promotions involving quick conversions: flash sales, limited-time offers, and the like.

Transform: Incorporating a reward into your offers for sharing your promotion with followers can broaden your reach quickly. 🧘

A Quick Look at Two More Specialty Social Media Platforms

Imgur

Why Bother?

Imgur, which has been called "Pinterest for guys," is an image-sharing platform (think photos and GIFs) that allows users to vote posts up in popularity. Its user base is especially tilted toward Millennial males. As of December 2014 it had 150 million users with 5.5 billion monthly page views and 1.5 million images uploaded daily. Its users are 81 percent male, and 72 percent are thirty-four or younger.

The Basics

Because of Imgur's user experience, in which posts are voted up or down, organic marketing probably won't be very effective here—Imgur's Millennial-heavy audience is especially sensitive to explicit marketing. But marketers can advertise to Imgur's audience via promoted posts that users recognize as marketing but are less likely to be offended by.

One example of a successful Imgur marketing effort was an Old Spice campaign that featured animated GIFs and content aimed specifically at Imgur's audience. The campaign launched with this message: "Hello Imgur, it's us—Old Spice. After millions of hours spent enjoying your GIF wars, confession bears, and how-to posts, we wanted to deliver a special something for your gray matter to process: our very own GIF Off."

The campaign featured GIFs of characters Old Spice had been using in television spots, all competing over which fragrance was better. Imgur users were receptive to the marketing message and approach—the "GIF off"—because it appealed to their sensibilities. One commenter on the app wrote, "The beautiful bastards in your marketing department understand me better than any man." Another said, "I never thought I'd find myself saying this, but this is the kind of shameless ad posting I can get behind. #teamtimber."

LINE

Why Bother?

LINE is an app developed and popularized in Japan for texts, images, and audio as well as free VoIP (Voice over Internet Protocol) telephone calls and teleconferences. LINE has 560 million registered users, with 205 million active monthly users. Only 25 million of those users are in the United States, so LINE is for marketers looking to reach a primarily Japanese audience—at least for now.

The Basics

LINE has been called a "closed social media platform," as it allows users to post the sort of message they would normally share on social media but only send it to the people they want to see it. As LINE's U.S. CEO Jeanie Han described the platform, "LINE is more than a messaging app. It's sort of like social media but it's not too open. It's just enough for people to feel comfortable. You get to choose how you want to communicate with your friends and family. You have complete control over that. You don't have to worry about your picture being taken last night and now the whole world is going to see it."

To market on LINE, you first set up an official account for your brand. LINE includes a feature called stickers, similar to emojis, which brands can custom create. Brands such as McDonald's have begun offering coupons on LINE, as well.

Summing It Up: Do's and Don'ts for Secondary Social Media Platforms

DON'T get overwhelmed by the number of social media platforms out there when deciding where to spend your time and money.

DO familiarize yourself with each of the different platforms and understand where your audience is spending *their* time. And if you are seeking a particular demographic, do some research—you might find a platform where your audience is already there and waiting for you.

> "Advertising is the ability to sense, interpret...to put the very heart throbs of a business into type, paper, and ink."
>
> Leo Burnett

Social Advertising
Facebook Ads, Sponsored Tweets, and More

SO, YOU'VE INVESTED A HUGE AMOUNT of time and effort into organic social media marketing. You've polished your company's profiles and pages, you've come up with strategies for the channels where your target audience spends their time, and you're posting engaging content on a regular basis.

Now you're supposed to start paying for social media ads, too?!

Here's the thing: social media marketing used to be all about the free stuff. Marketers didn't really use paid advertising all that much, because (1) they didn't need to, with the reach they got organically, and (2) it didn't work all that well anyway. But, over the years, that situation has gradually changed. Social advertising got better and better at helping marketers reach exactly the right audience, with impressive results, and, at least on Facebook, organic reach declined dramatically for businesses, due to pesky algorithm changes aimed at—what else?—moving marketers toward paid advertising options.

155

At Marketing Zen, we've found that the most effective social media marketing strategy today is a combination of organic and paid approaches. The day-to-day maintenance of an organic presence on Facebook, Twitter, and any other platform where your audience hangs out is vital to building a relationship with them—but the best way to get your brand in front of that audience in the first place, hands down, is to use paid advertising.

Advertising powerhouse Facebook goes out of its way to help marketers get great results from their paid ad campaigns, providing businesses with an unprecedented ability to target any demographic they want, customize campaigns based on their objectives, carefully track how effective an ad is via analytics, and make necessary changes in real time. Twitter isn't far behind with the extensive advertising capabilities it offers, and Pinterest and Instagram are also respectable players in the field.

Let's take a look at how to set up a paid ad campaign on each of these four platforms.

Facebook

Before we start talking about Facebook advertising, let's take a quick look at exactly how many people are on this social media giant. Facebook has more than 1.49 billion active monthly users and 1.31 billion active monthly mobile users. Now consider this: according to *Adweek*, in 2015, 56 percent of Facebook users reported clicking on an ad.

That's pretty huge, wouldn't you say?

Now imagine that out of those millions willing to click on an ad, you could single out the precise consumers you wanted to reach. Married moms in their thirties who live in Texas and are interested in technology? No problem. Urban Millennials who are into yoga and make a lot of purchases online? You got it.

Yes, it's annoying that Facebook has now, for all intents and purposes, become a "pay-to-play" platform for marketers. But they have definitely made it worth your while. Their advertising platform *will* get your message noticed by the audience you specify—all you have to do is create the perfect ad campaign.

So how do you do that, you ask? Let's walk through the process together.

1. **Get familiar with the Facebook Business Manager.** Navigate over to http://business.facebook.com to create your Facebook Business Manager account. The Business Manager is your one-stop shop for managing all your ad accounts, Facebook pages, and Facebook apps. It's through the Business Manager that you can access the two advertising tools Facebook provides—the Facebook Ads Manager and the Facebook Power Editor—to create your ads. It gives you an overview of your spending and your impressions, along with metrics on each specific page and ad account. The Business Manager even allows you to provide access to multiple people and third-party agencies to manage your Facebook assets and still keep those assets secure. Time spent learning how to use this tool to your advantage will pay off when you start running ads.

2. **Choose your advertising tool.** For most marketers and most situations, the Facebook Ads Manager is the best choice for creating and managing ad campaigns. It allows you to create and run ads, target your ads to your desired audience, set a budget for each campaign, monitor the performance of your campaigns, and manage the billing for your campaigns.

   However, for marketers looking for an even higher level of control over multiple ad campaigns, the Facebook Power Editor might be the right choice. It includes search and filter features, as well as ad creation and editing abilities that cater to businesses that have large marketing departments and often run multiple Facebook ad campaigns at once.

   As we go through the ad creation process, I'll be focusing on the Facebook Ads Manager as the most common choice.

3. **Decide on the objective of your ad campaign.** What exactly do you want your ad campaign to achieve? Under the Campaign tab, Facebook allows you to choose from objectives such as increasing conversions, sending traffic to your website, promoting your Facebook page, and boosting installs of your app, just to name a few.

Let's say we're running an ad to drive traffic to our website. We'd choose "Send people to your website," and then enter the web address where we want to send our audience. At this point, Facebook gives you the opportunity to create a Facebook pixel to track the website traffic your ad generates; you'll definitely want to take advantage of this feature. See step 11 below for more about pixels!

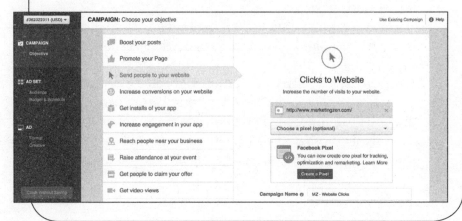

4. **Choose the demographic you're targeting with your campaign.** In the Ad Set tab, you'll decide who exactly your audience will be. For our example campaign, I've selected everyone aged eighteen and up all across the United States, but you can target people in any location, age group, or gender, and even narrow it down by language, as well.

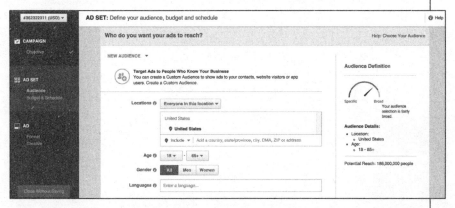

5. **Narrow your audience even further.** In the Detailed Targeting section, you can get even more specific with the demographic you want to reach by adding the interests and behaviors you'd like your audience members to exhibit. You can also exclude certain segments of users within your chosen demographic. Facebook collects a large amount of data on its users to ensure these ads are targeted appropriately, but it also employs information from data brokers such as Acxiom, Datalogix, and Epsilon, which keep profiles that tie back to individual Facebook users and include their online activity across the entire internet.

Once you've homed in on your ideal audience, you can save that demographic under a specific Audience Name for use in future ad campaigns.

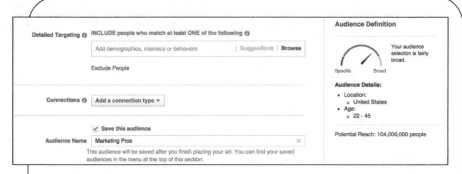

6. Set your budget. In the next section of the Ad Set tab, you'll decide on your campaign budget and schedule.

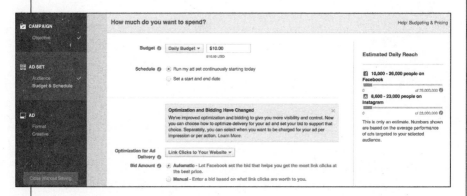

You can customize the delivery of your ads to change when you get charged, and when your ads will be shown.

7. **Start creating your ad!** In the Ad tab, you'll decide how you want your ad to look, and upload the necessary creatives. You can use carousel or single image ads on Facebook or, alternatively, videos!

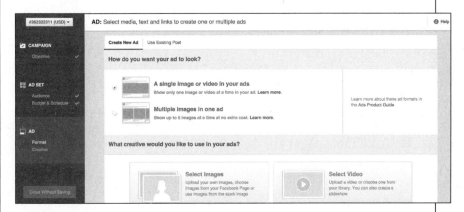

8. **Choose where your ad will appear.** Your options? Desktop, Mobile, Desktop Right Column, and/or (newly added) Instagram!

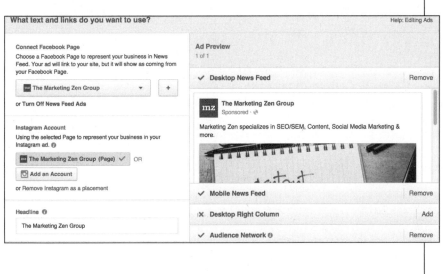

9. **Input your ad copy.** You'll write your headline, ad text, and call to action here.

Headline *ⓘ*

> The Marketing Zen Group

Text *ⓘ*

> Marketing Zen specializes in SEO/SEM, Content, Social Media Marketing & more.

Call-to-Action Button *ⓘ*

> Learn More ▾

Show Advanced Options ▾

10. **Preview how your ad will appear.** Finally, you can double-check that everything looks good in each different ad location you choose, before placing your order!

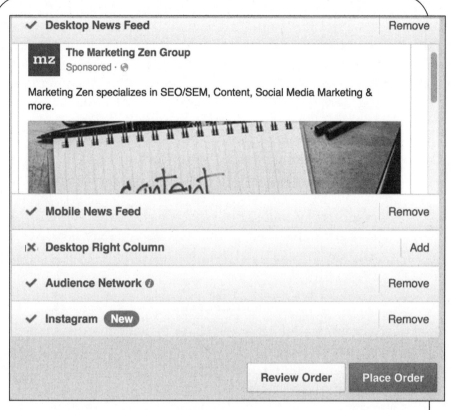

11. **Get familiar with pixels!** Now that your campaign is up and running, you'll want to track its performance. Google Analytics is unable to track website traffic coming from Facebook campaigns, so Facebook offers marketers "conversion pixels" that can be placed on any webpage to track conversions from ad campaigns. For example, if the ad's objective is to drive sales, the conversion pixel should be placed on the page your website visitor lands on after making a purchase, such as a Thank You or confirmation page. This will enable you to keep tabs on how well your ad campaign is working.

While we're on the subject of pixels, I'd be remiss if I didn't mention another kind of pixel Facebook offers: their retargeting, or audience, pixel. You can place Facebook "audience pixels" on your website to track visitors who also happen to be Facebook users—and then create custom audiences made up of these visitors to retarget with your Facebook ads. Retargeting is a great way to stay top of mind for people who have recently visited your website. Maybe they read a few blog posts, or checked out a few products, and then left … but later, if they log on to Facebook and see your brand again, they might just decide to go ahead and make that purchase then.

These pixels even allow specific audience segmentation by various website behaviors, such as visiting specific pages on your website or visiting your website but not returning for a specified amount of time. You can create entire Facebook ad campaigns targeting your website visitors based on behavior, moving them along the sales funnel more quickly than ever before.

Instagram

OK, guys, brace yourselves: I'm about to launch into a detailed, in-depth explanation of paid Instagram advertising. Are you ready? Are you sure? OK, here goes.

See above.

Yep, since Facebook owns Instagram, the ad platforms are the same for both. So if you can put together a Facebook ad campaign, you can handle Instagram, too.

There are a few minor differences for Instagram, such as a shorter list of ad objectives to choose from, but, other than that, it's essentially the same. Instagram ads are even created within Facebook's Ads Manager. Excitingly, Instagram campaigns can also be run on Facebook, in the same way that organic Instagram posts can be shared on Facebook—and those all-important conversion pixels work for Instagram campaigns, as well.

Twitter

Twitter isn't far behind Facebook when it comes to making paid advertising worthwhile for companies. While Twitter's organic reach for businesses is still intact, the benefits of being able to target a specific audience with a particular ad are extremely attractive. And now that Twitter doesn't only offer Promoted Tweets and Promoted Trends anymore but has introduced new ad types into the mix—such as video ads, popular with mobile users, and "shoppable tweets" with a Buy button built right in—more and more businesses are taking note.

Here's how you can put together your own Twitter ad campaign.

1. **Log in to the Twitter advertising platform.** Head over to http://ads.twitter.com to launch your Twitter campaign.

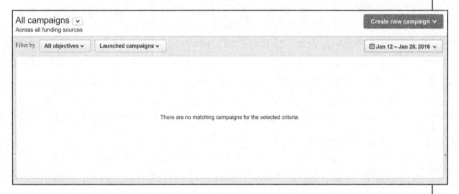

2. **Choose the objective of your campaign.** In the top right-hand corner of the dashboard, click on "Create a new campaign," and choose the objective of the campaign. These objectives range from increasing followers to boosting website clicks to finding leads on Twitter.

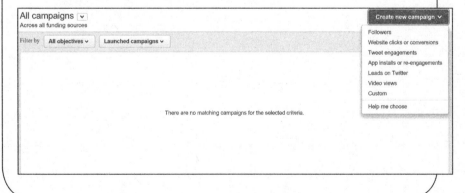

3. **Set up your campaign basics.** Next, you'll need to name your campaign, and decide when you want it to run.

4. **Choose your target demographic.** As with Facebook, you can choose your audience based on demographic information such as location and gender, as well as more detailed data like interests and behavior. You can even choose to target followers of specific industry influencers or competitors on Twitter—something my team at Marketing Zen has experienced great results with.

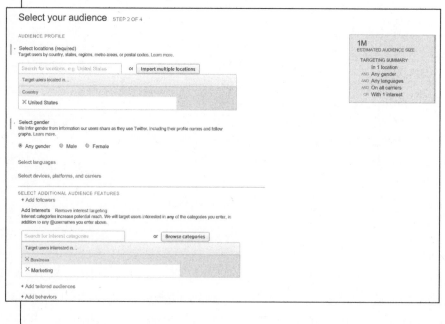

5. **Set your budget.** Here you'll have the opportunity to set your daily budget as well as your overall budget for the campaign.

6. **Create your ad!** Upload your creatives and enter your ad copy to create your new ad. Alternatively, you can choose to use an already existing, published tweet in your campaign, instead.

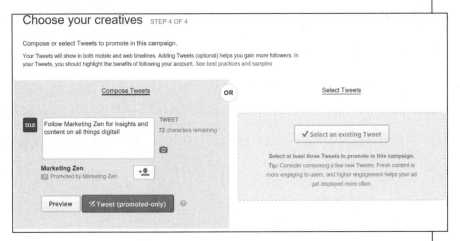

7. **Launch your campaign!** Once your ad is ready to go, scroll back up to the top of the dashboard and click "Launch."

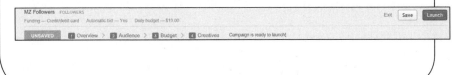

Once your campaign has launched, be sure to keep an eye out for a sudden explosion of followers from a different country, off-topic comments in broken English or even in other languages, or negative, harassing comments—these spammy responses need to be addressed quickly. Revise your targeting, or report or respond to negative comments, to salvage the situation.

Pinterest

Even though Pinterest isn't owned by Twitter, the two platforms have remarkably similar advertising options. Promoted pins are the primary way to advertise on Pinterest, and, just like Twitter, Pinterest has also recently rolled out "shoppable pins" with Buy buttons built in. The highly visual social media platform made many exciting announcements for businesses in early 2016 and has released some impressive numbers as a friendly reminder of how the platform continues to gain popularity year after year.

Here's how to set up your Pinterest ad campaign to increase brand awareness, engagement, and, most importantly, conversions.

1. **Decide on your objective.** I recommend choosing the objective of sending visits to your website. Your Pinterest engagement—people following your boards and commenting on and re-pinning your pins—will skyrocket as well, but it'll be free: you'll only pay for clicks.

Boost engagement with your Pins

Track your audience's signals of intent. You get charged for each engagement (closeup, repin, click) on your Pin.

Get traffic to your website

Send a motivated audience to your content. You get charged for clicks to your website.

Cancel   Pick a Pin

2. **Set your budget.** There's no minimum to promote a pin, and the total cost of your campaign will vary depending on your targeted audience and your bid. Your campaigns only cost you, however, when someone clicks on or engages with the promoted pin by commenting or liking it (depending on the objective you chose above).

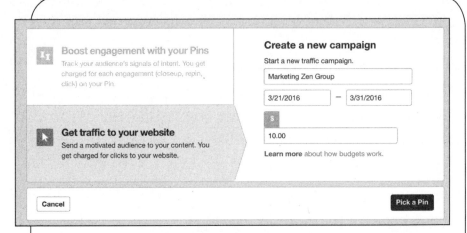

3. **Pick your pin.** Unlike Facebook, Twitter, and Instagram, only existing pins can be used in a Pinterest ad. This means that you'll need to create the pin you'll be using as an ad and pin it to a board before setting up your campaign.

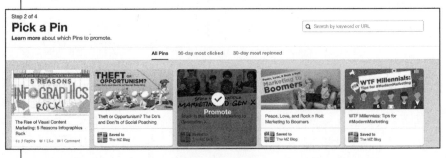

4. **Choose your target demographic.** Pinterest allows you to narrow your ad's audience by interest.

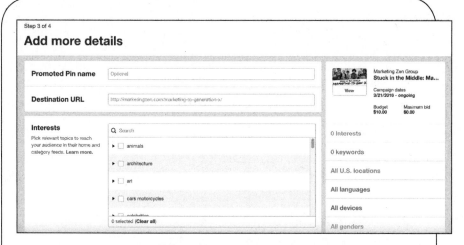

Add more details

Promoted Pin name — Optional

Destination URL — http://marketingzen.com/marketing-to-generation-x/

Interests
Pick relevant topics to reach your audience in their home and category feeds. Learn more.

Search
- animals
- architecture
- art
- cars motorcycles
- celebrities

0 selected (Clear all)

Marketing Zen Group
Stuck in the Middle: Ma...
Campaign dates
3/21/2016 - ongoing

Budget — $10.00
Maximum bid — $0.00

0 interests
0 keywords
All U.S. locations
All languages
All devices
All genders

5. **Add keywords.** Along with a visual element and a caption, promoted pins allow you to associate around 150 hidden keywords with the pin. In choosing your keywords, take advantage of research you've done for other marketing efforts, such as SEO for your website and paid search campaigns. Do keep in mind, however, that Pinterest has to approve your ad and will likely reject attempts to stuff the ad with irrelevant keywords.

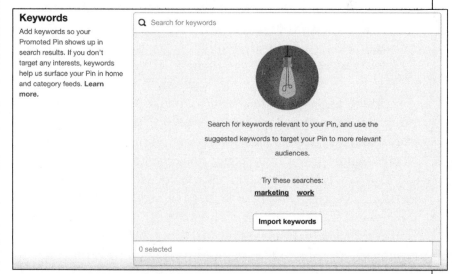

Keywords

Add keywords so your Promoted Pin shows up in search results. If you don't target any interests, keywords help us surface your Pin in home and category feeds. **Learn more.**

Search for keywords

Search for keywords relevant to your Pin, and use the suggested keywords to target your Pin to more relevant audiences.

Try these searches:
marketing   **work**

Import keywords

0 selected

Use your keywords to target shoppers on Pinterest who are searching for specific phrases. For example, a retailer focusing on women's clothing could choose to target users searching for "women's summer dresses" or "girls' tops."

6. **Narrow your target audience down further.** Pinterest allows you to select your audience using four criteria: location, language, device, and gender.

Locations	● All U.S. locations ○ Pick specific locations
Languages	● All languages ○ Pick specific languages
Devices	● All devices ○ Pick specific devices
Genders	● All genders ○ Pick specific genders

7. **Track your campaign's performance with pixels.** Like Facebook, Pinterest offers a conversion pixel you can use to track conversions through your promoted pins. And as with any ads, comments may rack up under your promoted pin. Make sure these comments are being monitored and that you're responding to them if necessary.

As much as people think of social media as a platform for organic marketing, your business simply can't afford to ignore its paid advertising capabilities—especially in the case of Facebook, where organic reach is basically nonexistent. But be careful to spend your advertising dollars wisely. Focus your advertising efforts on the platform where your audience is most active, and think about the reason your audience visits that social platform. Is it to shop? To get inspiration? To learn something? Use those insights to cater to your audience by designing ads that address those reasons, and you'll see amazing results.

"Online video production will account for more than **one-third** of all online advertising spending within the next five years."

Borrell Associates

Video
A Powerful Social Medium

My #1 source for online video information is Dave Kaminski of Web Video University (www.WebVideoUniversity.com). Dave teaches thousands of people online how to create successful online videos through his training programs. He is the expert when it comes to this area, so I have asked him to write this guest chapter.

On April 23, 2005, a video was uploaded to the internet. It was titled "Meet Me at the Zoo." It was nineteen seconds long, and it featured elephants because of their "really, really, really long trunks." That was the very first video uploaded to YouTube.

Today, 500 hours of video are uploaded to YouTube every minute.

Back then, videos were standard definition, very poor quality, fewer than ten minutes long, and suffered from constant pausing or freezing during playback.

Today, videos can be as high as 8K (eight times the quality of full HD) and three-hour movies are streamed perfectly and without interruption to small mobile devices.

Back then, video was shot using cameras that required physical tapes. If you shot thirty minutes of video, it would take you thirty minutes to transfer it to your computer before you could even edit it.

Today, video shot on a smartphone can not only be seen by the world moments after it was created . . . it also can be streamed live at any time, too.

> Crafted intelligently, web video is a brilliant viral tool to attract, engage, and convert viewers to take action better than any other marketing medium on the web.
>
> Sherman Hu,
> *ShermanLive.com*

In short, web video has become the fastest-growing form of media in the history of the world. But what started as a novelty has now become commonplace, even expected. For businesses, web video is now just as important as a website and a phone number.

But what if you don't have any videos for your business, or aren't happy with the ones you have? Well, that's what this chapter is all about: how to do video the right way for your business.

And what you'll be learning here isn't based on theory or because "everyone says to do it." Rather, it's based on my experience of making, marketing, and profiting from web video since before YouTube even existed. So let's get started.

The Equipment You Need for Making Videos

I've taught tens of thousands of people how to make videos for the web. And if there's one thing they always want to know first, it's what stuff they should use to make their videos. So I thought it would make sense to start here first.

A word of caution, though. Technology changes fast. In fact, changes in technology are a big reason why web video has exploded. So keep in mind that the recommendations I make here are often general, but when I do recommend a specific piece of equipment, there may be something newer out there by the time you read this.

Cameras

There's a saying that the best camera is the one you have with you at the moment. And for the most part, it's true.

Any camera these days will be good enough for web video. It will shoot HD video that is perfectly fine for YouTube, marketing videos, training videos, or whatever else you plan to shoot. Smartphones, action cameras, DSLRs (digital single-lens reflex cameras), point-and-shoots . . . if it was made in the past couple years, the quality of your videos will be absolutely fine.

The only major difference between all of the camera choices out there really comes down to one major thing: workflow. And by that, I mean how quickly you can shoot, edit, and get your videos on the web.

For instance, a smartphone can be great for quick, on-the-go videos, such as interviewing someone at an event or sharing a quick tip with your audience. But it will slow your workflow down if you're making a series of thirty training videos. In fact, you may not even be able to fit all of that footage on your smartphone.

So I prepared the little checklist below, showing you which camera option will work best with which type of video:

Smartphones—Good for quick, on-the-go videos shot in natural daylight. Bad for longer or multiple videos and where artificial lighting has to be used.

Action Cameras (think GoPro)—Good for wide shots, action shots, and videos where you are showing things as they happen. Bad for talking head–type videos or videos that require artificial light.

Point-and-Shoot Cameras (designed only for photos/video and with the lens built in)—Good for virtually any type of video. Bad when good audio is important.

DSLR Cameras (those pro-looking photo cameras with removable lenses)—Good, actually great, for virtually any type of video. Bad because people are intimidated by them.

Traditional Video Cameras (any of the options not listed above)—Good for any type of video. Bad because you'll have a harder time finding them these days, and eventually they'll become extinct.

Do I have a personal favorite among these? Yep, DSLR cameras. They are the only type of camera I use for 99 percent of my videos. Why? Because you get Hollywood-level quality and lots of flexibility, and they are terrific in low light. But on the downside, you do have to get past your fear of all those buttons.

Oh, and one more thing: It's always best to use a camera that gives you the ability to plug in an external microphone. Using a camera's built-in microphone almost always gives you poor audio quality. Plugging in an external microphone fixes that. Which leads us to the next section . . .

Audio

Having good audio is just as important as having good video. In fact, it's more important. Studies have shown that people will watch a video that has good audio longer than one that doesn't. And for good audio, we'll plug a microphone into our camera (or computer). Here are your choices.

Shotgun Mic—This is a microphone that sits on top of your camera and looks a little like a hot dog. It will do a better job than your camera's built-in mic of capturing all of the audio in the area you are recording, which means it is ideal for capturing audio when more than one person is speaking on camera. The drawbacks with a shotgun mic are that you must be fairly close to the camera, usually within ten feet, and it will pick up background noise (think birds chirping or dogs barking).

A good shotgun mic for most cameras is the Rode VideoMic.

A good shotgun mic for smartphones is the Ampridge MightyMic.

Lavalier Mic—This is a microphone that plugs into your camera, while the other end (the microphone part) is attached to your shirt, usually around your chest. Lavalier or "lav" mics typically produce the best-sounding audio, hands down, and do a great job of eliminating any background noise. Their main purpose is to record the voice of a single person speaking on camera. However, if you want to record multiple people speaking on camera at once, a lavalier mic won't be your best choice. Go with a shotgun mic instead. Lavalier mics are available in both wired and wireless versions, but wireless lavalier mics cost considerably more.

A good, cheap, wired lavalier mic for most cameras is the Audio-Technica ATR-3350.

A good, but not cheap, wireless lavalier mic for most cameras is the Sennheiser EW 100 G3.

A good, wired lavalier microphone for smartphones is the Rode smartLav+.

USB Condenser Mic—This microphone is used for recording audio on your computer, not on your camera. For example, you would use it if you were recording a screencast (video of what you're doing on your computer screen). It is plug and play; you simply plug it into a USB port on your computer and you instantly have great audio. There is nothing to install, configure, or mess with. And they work equally well on both Windows and Macs.

A good USB condenser mic is the Blue Yeti.

Another good USB condenser mic is the Blue Nessie.

And yet another good USB condenser mic is the Audio-Technica AT2020 USB.

Video Editing Software

Once you have your video shot, you're going to need to edit it. You'll cut out mistakes, add graphics, or adjust the colors. What software you choose for editing mostly depends on what type of computer you use, Windows or Mac. But be clear on one thing: all video editing software does the same thing—it allows you to edit your video. So don't get caught up thinking one title is necessarily better than another. It doesn't work that way. What video editing software someone uses is based more on personal preference than a feature set.

Sony Vegas—If you're a Windows user, Sony Vegas is probably going to be not only the cheapest solution but the easiest to start using. You can start with their low-priced "studio" version and upgrade to more feature-rich versions whenever you're ready.

Adobe Premiere Elements—If you're a Mac user, Premiere Elements is an inexpensive and easy way to edit most videos on a Mac. Please note the Premiere Elements is also available for Windows, but Sony Vegas is the better choice.

Adobe Premiere Pro—This is truly feature-rich video editing software available for both Windows and Mac users. It gives you everything you need when starting out, plus everything you could ever possibly need in the future. But it's only available as part of Adobe's Creative Cloud subscription service, which means you'll need to pay Adobe a very reasonable monthly fee to use it. If you're serious about sticking with video for the long term, investing in Adobe Premiere Pro will be your smartest choice.

Screen Recording Software

There are two types of videos you can make for the web: on-camera video and screencast video. With a screencast video you are recording what you're doing on your computer screen (for example, a video of how you research vacation hot spots using your browser). And to make these screencast videos, you need a different type of software called *screen recording software*. The good news is there are clear choices for both Windows and Mac users. Here they are:

Camtasia—If you're a Windows user, Camtasia is your best choice. It's a little expensive but has been the number-one choice of screencast video creators for over a decade. It's relatively simple to use, it's feature rich, and it just works. As an added bonus, it can be used to edit regular video, too. It can pull double-duty; it can be used *both* as video editing software and screencast software. But as video editing software, it is weak when compared to Sony Vegas or Adobe Premiere Pro. So most regular video makers use it only for making screencast videos.

ScreenFlow—If you're a Mac user, ScreenFlow is your best choice. It's inexpensive and is the number-one choice for screencast video makers on a Mac. It's a joy to use and is very stable. Just like Camtasia, it can be used to edit regular video, too. This means it can also pull double-duty as both video editing software and screencast software. But also like Camtasia, as video editing software it is weak when compared to Adobe Premiere Elements or Adobe Premiere Pro.

Video Lights

All video cameras perform best when you shoot using natural daylight. But natural daylight will not always be available for every video you shoot. In those cases, you're going to need to add artificial light to your videos. And no, light from your desk lamp won't do.

Instead you're going to need to use lights made specifically for video. And you'll quickly discover that there are lots of choices (at lots of different prices). So let me make it easy for you by telling you what to use and what to avoid.

LED (Light-Emitting Diode) or Tungsten Lights—LED are the newest lights and tungsten are the oldest lights. You'll want to avoid both of these. Why? Tungsten lights are hot and dangerous (and old). LED lights are unflattering. The light is harsh and the color is usually off. One day LED lights will be the best choice, but right now they still have some growing up to do.

Fluorescent Softbox Lights—These are the lights you want to use. First, they use fluorescent bulbs, which are cool, use little power, and will make you look your best. And second, they are goof-proof. You just plug them in and you'll have near perfect light. The secret is in the "softbox" part of the light, a tent-like box that wraps around the fluorescent bulbs. Its job is to soften the light and reduce shadows. The end result is that you look good, and all you had to do was turn on the light.

Is there a specific fluorescent softbox brand to get? Nope. Here's why: almost all video lights are made at the same factories in China. They just get different names slapped on them. So any fluorescent softbox light you find on eBay or Amazon will be perfectly fine. Just be aware that they are often sold in kits of two or three lights. And this is fine, as having an extra softbox light or two around is a good thing.

Is there a proper way to position a fluorescent softbox light for shooting video? Yes. Place it directly behind the camera, slightly higher than your head level and angled slightly down toward you or your subject. That's it. That was easy, huh?

All About YouTube

I'm going to start this section on YouTube by telling you something you're probably not expecting. And that is, YouTube doesn't work for every business. It used to be that you could upload a video to YouTube, using the keyword you were targeting for the title, and you'd be immediately ranked on the first page of YouTube. It meant that any business could get eyeballs on any video just by uploading something and entering a few words. It doesn't work that way anymore. Not even close.

These days YouTube is all about viewer engagement (which I'll talk more about in a bit). But for some business owners, that means if people aren't interested in your video topic, not only will your videos never be watched, but they'll never be found. For example, consider a video about your boring business trip to Lincoln, Nebraska: there's no audience for that. Unfortunately, that's the exact model most business owners follow with their YouTube marketing plans; they upload videos based on topics that they think people will be interested in. And then they wonder why they fail.

Don't do that. You've got to be a little more savvy. YouTube is a vast ocean of endless videos about anything and everything. Most are never even seen. In this section, I'm going to give you some tips to make sure your YouTube video efforts aren't wasted, as well as information about where your videos will be seen and where those views can ultimately get you traffic, leads, and sales. You ready? Here we go.

Channel focus: Every user on YouTube has their own channel. And your channel needs to be focused on just one topic. For example, if your business is teaching people urban gardening, then every video on your channel should be about urban gardening.

Too often people mix videos into their channel that are completely off topic. So maybe that channel about urban gardening contains videos about a new vacuum cleaner they love, a trip they took to Boston, or their dogs playing in the park. Suddenly that channel about urban gardening becomes a channel about . . . well, no one is really sure.

And if no one is really sure what your channel is about, then they won't be sure what your business is about either. In other words, you wouldn't send mixed messages about your business in other forms of marketing, so why would you on YouTube?

And the reasons why this channel focus is so important on YouTube will become even more clear in the next section.

It's all about subscribers and engagement: First let's talk about subscribers. These are the people who subscribe to your channel. Think of it like a mailing or lead list. Except you can't send mass emails to these people; rather, they are your "fans" and are notified whenever you post new videos.

Building your channel subscriber count is critical on YouTube for two reasons. First, YouTube rewards channels with larger subscriber counts more than it rewards channels with lower subscriber counts. For example, if a channel with no subscribers posts a video and a channel with many subscribers posts a nearly identical video, the channel with many subscribers will have their video rank higher, at least initially, and often long term.

Why? Because YouTube wants its visitors to stay on YouTube. That's how they make money. And a channel with an established audience will likely bring in more money for them than a channel that no one really seems interested in. So right off the bat, channels with lots of subscribers always get their videos ranked higher in search results.

And the second reason for building your channel subscribers is video views. With more subscribers, you'll get more video views. Automatically. More video views will in turn grow your video rankings and ultimately your subscriber count.

Let me go back to the example I gave earlier, where nearly identical videos were posted by a channel with no subscribers and one with many. The only way that channel with no subscribers will get any video views is if people find the video while searching. On the other hand, the channel with many subscribers will instantly receive views for their video *because all of their existing subscribers will be notified about the video*. See how that works?

Another very important factor in getting videos ranked is engagement, which means how people interact with your videos. Engagement includes views, comments, shares, and whether your YouTube video gets viewers to watch another YouTube video.

The basic premise is that the more engagement a video has, the more popular it must be, and therefore the better ranking YouTube will give it.

In fact, engagement on a video is often a more important ranking factor than the size of the channel that published it. So, for example, while a channel with no subscribers will initially be beaten by a channel with many subscribers, it can turn the tables by producing a video that gets more engagement. This is why you'll sometimes see a video from a tiny channel ranking number one for a search term, while videos from giant channels are ranked below it. The video from the tiny channel has more engagement, and YouTube rewards them for it.

But if you're just starting out, or you have an existing channel that might as well be dead, how do you go about building subscribers and getting engagement? I lay it all out for you in the next sections.

Keywords *Before* Videos

I want you to burn this rule into your brain. You identify keywords first and then make your videos based on those keywords. You never just make videos about what you think people will be interested in.

Here's why.

If you're new on YouTube or have an existing channel with few subscribers, the only way people will ever find you is through searches. And if your videos are not targeting the keywords people search for, no one will ever find you.

An example of the right way to do this: You identify the keyword phrase "tape golfer's elbow." You then make a video about how to apply tape to someone who has golfer's elbow. You then give the video the title "A Quick and Easy Way to Tape Golfer's Elbow."

Because people are actively searching for "tape golfer's elbow" and because your video title contains "tape golfer's elbow" and because your video is 100 percent on topic, people will find your video, you'll get views, and you'll hopefully get engagement and subscribers.

An example of the wrong way to do this: You decide to make a video about a new golf club you bought, because you believe people will think it's cool. You title your video "Testing Out My New Driver at Shady Farm."

Because no one is searching for any words in that title, no one will find you. And you'll get no views (other than family and friends), no engagement, and no subscribers.

Unfortunately, the wrong way is exactly what most business owners do on YouTube. So let's learn how to do it right.

For keyword research, you don't need any special tools, just

Google and YouTube. You'll start off on Google first, typing in a general keyword for which your market might search. But instead of looking at the search results, you'll go to the bottom of the page and look at Google's listing of related searches. That's where the keyword gold mine is found.

For example, I might search Google for "golfer's elbow." I jump to the bottom of the results page and look at Google's listing for "searches related to golfer's elbow." I see things like "golfer's elbow treatment" and "golfer's elbow stretches." You might find a great keyword right then and there. Or you might need to click on one of the related searches and repeat the process. In which case, you might find the keyword "golfer's elbow stretching exercises."

Now you'll jump over to YouTube and search for that phrase.

This is what you're looking for: On the first page of results, the majority of the videos have thousands or tens of thousands of views. If there are a few videos that have hundreds, hundreds of thousands, or even millions of views, that's fine, too.

What these numbers are telling us is that there is plenty of traffic for that search term on YouTube and that keyword is not dominated by big channels. In other words, we have a good chance of landing on the first page and getting some eyeballs on our videos.

This is what you're not looking for: On the first page of the results, the majority of the videos have hundreds of thousands or millions of views or the majority of the videos only have hundreds of views.

What these numbers are telling us is that either that keyword is too competitive and we'll never rank for it, or there simply isn't enough search volume to make it worth our while.

You're going to repeat this process until you come up with five keyword phrases for your market. And these five keyword phrases must be unrelated. For example, I would come up with five keyword phrases related to golf health and conditioning, not five keyword phrases related to golfer's elbow.

Why these five keyword phrases? Because we're going to test and probe the market on YouTube. We don't know which of these keyword phrases will bring us lots of viewers/subscribers and which ones might be duds. And the only way you will ever know is by making some videos, uploading them, and viewing the results.

That means it's time to make our videos. And we'll do it using a specific formula.

The YouTube Video Formula

When we make our videos for YouTube, we're going to follow a formula that goes like this:

1. Our video content is made specifically for the keyword we're targeting.
2. At the start of the video, we state the viewer's problem and promise a fix.
3. We display a three- to four-second "bumper," which is just our logo/tagline/website.
4. We deliver the content, which is the "fix" for the viewer's "problem."
5. We specifically ask the viewer to engage with our video.
6. When we upload our video, we'll put the keyword phrase in the title.

Six steps to the formula. That's it. Even better, none of these steps are hard. So let's take a closer look at each step.

1. Our video content is made specifically for the keyword we're targeting: This is a no-brainer. If my keyword is "golfer's elbow stretching exercises," then my video is going to be all about exercises for golfer's elbow. In other words, your content must 100 percent match the keyword you're targeting.

2. At the start of the video, we state the viewer's problem and promise a fix: Most people stumble at the beginning of their videos or play some fancy animation. But the beginning of the video is where we'll either draw viewers in or make them click away. So we want to tell them what's in store for them by watching our video. Remind them why they clicked play and what they are going to receive. And the best way to do this is to state the problem they are facing and promise them a fix to it in the video.

3. **We display a three- to four-second "bumper," which is just our logo/tagline/website:** This brief bit is meant as a segue between stating the problem and giving them our actual video content (the fix to the problem). This "bumper," as it's called, is usually only three or four seconds long and is a full-screen graphic or animation with music in the background, displaying your tagline, your business name, your website, or even all of them at once.

4. **We deliver the content, which is the "fix" for the viewer's "problem":** No special rules here. This is your content. This is what your video is all about. So if I were making a video targeting "golfer's elbow stretching exercises," this is where I'd talk about and demonstrate those exercises.

5. **We specifically ask the viewer to engage with our video:** This part is critical. Like, really, really critical. At the end of our video, we are specifically going to ask the viewer to subscribe to our channel and comment on our video. Something like, "If you enjoyed this video, it would really help me out if you would subscribe to my channel . . . and if you have any questions or thoughts, please leave them in the comments section below." Ridiculously simple, right? The only thing more ridiculous is how well it works. This step alone can grow your channel subscribers and video engagement by leaps and bounds.

6. **When we upload our video, we'll put the keyword phrase in the title:** When you upload your videos to YouTube, you can add a title, description, tags, and more. The title of your video is king, the most important, the one you want to focus on. Initially, it's what YouTube will use to determine what your video is about (after that, they look at engagement). So you must have your keyword phrase in the title, but you want to sprinkle other

words around it. So for "golfer's elbow stretching exercises," I might make my video title "3 Golfer's Elbow Stretching Exercises for Fast Pain Relief."

But how long should your video be? It used to be that you always wanted to keep your videos under two minutes, because you start losing viewers after that. But because engagement is such an important ranking factor on YouTube these days, longer videos can actually be better (the longer someone watches a video, the more engaged YouTube deems them to be).

So I recommend a happy medium, which means a video between two and six minutes long. A video in that range is short enough that it doesn't take you a long time to make, yet has enough length to score extra engagement points.

I also recommend that you upload all five of your videos at the same time. That way you can get a true head-to-head comparison on which keyword phrase performs the best.

When you follow this formula, what you'll typically see is that one keyword phrase stands out—it gets a lot more views than all the others. On the other end, there will be a keyword phrase that gets very few views. And the rest will be in the middle.

But once you know which keyword phrase is the winner, you go about creating even more videos around that specific topic. Fill your channel with lots of videos that people are searching for and want to see . . . rather than videos that no one ever watches.

And finally, you might be wondering how you'll get any viewers off of YouTube and onto your own website, where you can actually make money from them.

As long as you display your website in the bumper portion of the video, in the description for your video, or, better yet, at the end of the video (when you're telling people to subscribe and comment), people interested in your business will find you. Promise.

What About Using Videos On Your Website or Blog?

For many years, I recommended that people focus more on publishing videos to their own website or blog, rather than on

YouTube. And the reason was simple: videos on your own website could outrank videos on YouTube in the search engines.

That's not the case anymore. These days, videos on YouTube almost always outrank a video on your own website. For example, if you took the same video and published it to both YouTube and your blog at the same time, using the same titles, the video on YouTube will show up in the search engines way faster and way higher than the video on your blog.

In fact, Google now only displays video results in its search listings if the video is on YouTube or is on a "video site." What's a video site? It's a website where the content is 100 percent video. Which means your blog is not a video site.

So when it comes to using videos on your own website or blog, my recommendation is yes, absolutely use video when and where you can. Just don't expect to get a lot (or any) video-related search traffic from it.

Instead, use video as a tool to build authenticity and authority. It will keep your new and existing visitors coming back for more, ultimately becoming your clients or customers.

The Ultimate Teaching Tool

Want to know the most profitable way to use web video? Create video-based training courses, which is a collection of pre-recorded video lessons or webinars.

If there's one area where web video has created an entirely new market, it would be e-learning. When I started out with video online, I was one of a handful of people offering video training lessons. Today, it's an entire industry.

From mathematics, to cooking, to software coding, to marketing, to . . . well, anything you can think of, if there's an audience that wants to learn how to do it, there's an opportunity to develop and publish video training courses on it.

Why has video training become so popular? Because it's the ultimate teaching tool. Seeing how to do something is far more powerful than (and far superior to) reading about how to do something. If a picture is worth a thousand words, then a video is worth a million.

And producing video training can also be very lucrative. While some type of written training might sell for $10 to $50, video training on the same topics can often sell for $100 to $500. And the only "product" you need to deliver is a way for people to securely watch your videos online.

This is actually a big headache. There's a lot of tech and moving parts involved. Sometimes it's enough to keep people away from offering any type of video training product.

But because the market and the opportunity has become so big, more and more solutions to these headaches are popping up. So if you're at all interested in making video training courses, and you know exactly what you want to teach, but you have been turned off by "the tech" of actually selling and delivering your training course, here's a list of options that will make it easy for you:

Udemy—The largest marketplace for video training courses. You can find something for everyone. And you can publish and sell your own video training courses, too. *For free.* So what's the catch? Two big ones. First, Udemy is typically going to keep 50 percent of your sales for themselves. And second, someone who buys your training course won't be *your* customer; they will be a customer of Udemy, which means you can't market to them in the future. Which can lead to death for most businesses. Because of this Udemy "gotcha," a number of not-free solutions have emerged and the best are listed next.

Kajabi—Weird name, but it's an all-in-one-platform for people selling digital content, primarily video training courses. They do it all. They provide you with sales-page templates and a shopping cart; they host your videos and provide access for customers; they integrate with email services; and more. Basically, you just click your way to publishing and profiting from your video training course. The only drawback is the cost. Kajabi typically costs around $1,000 USD annually to use.

Teachable—Very similar to Kajabi, but not as refined. The big plus is cost; it can be far cheaper to use. The big minus is cash flow. You don't receive funds immediately after someone purchases your video training course. You have to wait thirty to sixty days before Teachable sends you the money.

Thinkific—Very similar to Teachable and Kajabi, but not as refined as either. The big pluses are cost (it can be far cheaper than Kajabi) and cash flow (you get your funds immediately, unlike Teachable). The big minus is the feature-set. It's just not quite as sophisticated as Teachable and offers far less in terms of features than you get with Kajabi.

Video Ads Even the Playing Field

Years ago, I used to be a big fan (and user) of paid advertising. Google AdWords (and all of their competitors) were responsible for driving large amounts of traffic to my sites. And the traffic was relatively cheap.

But that all changed when Google AdWords (and most of their competitors) started getting really expensive. Traffic that was costing 25 cents a click suddenly quadrupled or more. It drove many small-business owners (including myself) out of the paid advertising arena. There was no longer any good way to get cheap, targeted traffic.

Then along came video ads.

With video ads, you can once again get very cheap and very targeted traffic, at least for now. Part of the reason that video ads are so cheap is that video is a barrier. Anyone wanting to advertise has to make a video; they can't just type in some words and press go. With video advertising, the competition is also low, so low that there are plenty of markets that are virtually wide open.

So how and where do you run video ads? You have two options: YouTube and Facebook. Both are easy and both are cheap, but they are also different from each other.

YouTube Video Ads—With YouTube, your video ad will be a *pre-roll video*, which means your video ad will play before someone on YouTube can watch the video they clicked to watch. You've probably experienced this many times: You click to watch a video on YouTube, but a video ad plays first. And you have to wait at least five seconds before you can skip it. That's a pre-roll ad.

To run video ads on YouTube, you have to do it through a Google AdWords account. Yes, the same account used to run AdWords text-based ads is used to run YouTube video ads. That's both a good and bad thing: Good because AdWords is a very mature and feature-rich platform. Bad because your video ad must adhere to all of the same AdWords rules (and Google is notorious for being picky about what they do and don't allow with ads).

The other thing that catches people off guard is that your video ad must be a video that you've uploaded to your YouTube account. You can't give them just any video to run; it must be within your YouTube account.

In terms of targeting your video ads to a specific audience, you can target your ads based on demographics, keywords, and channels. Of those three, I would only recommend targeting channels (YouTube's demographics and keyword options are a bit lacking). By targeting channels, you can tell YouTube that you want your video ads to play for every video for a specific YouTube channel. For instance, you can target the channel of one of your competitors. Or the channels of the biggest movers and shakers in your market. Channel targeting is a powerful option and, again, the only option you should choose.

At the time of this writing, YouTube/Google will only charge you for a video ad if the viewer watches your video ad for more than thirty seconds or clicks on a link in your video ad. That's good news, because if people skip your ad or watch fewer than thirty seconds of it, you don't get charged.

Facebook Video Ads—Facebook is probably the biggest reason video ads are so cheap. They've given Google/YouTube the competition they've never had.

Unlike YouTube, Facebook ads are not pre-roll ads that people automatically see. Instead they are ads that appear in a Facebook user's news feed. And the user has to click the play button to actually see the video ad.

To run Facebook video ads, you just need a Facebook account. Within your account, you can access the Facebook Ads Manager where you can create both text and video ads on Facebook (and Instagram, too). Facebook walks you through the process step by step and, as a quick tip, it's best to use the Facebook "defaults" for the options they present (the defaults typically work best).

In terms of targeting, Facebook offers an insane amount of demographics. And this is where Facebook really shines, by allowing you to hyper-target your video ads based on a seemingly unlimited amount of demographic options.

At the time of this writing, Facebook charges you per impression. So if your ad appears in the news feed of a Facebook user, whether or not they even clicked to watch your video, you are charged. This is kind of a bummer because Facebook treats a video ad the same as a text ad, and they are very different things. I would expect Facebook to make some changes to this pricing structure in the future.

If you're just starting out and don't have a lot (or any) experience with video or paid ads in general, I'd recommend that you start with Facebook first. The Facebook ad system is a little easier to use than Google, and Facebook is a little more lenient with their ad guidelines.

But whichever platform you choose, always start small. Spend only $5 to $10 a day testing your video ads. Don't spend any more than that until you have solid numbers that indicate whether or not your video ads are bringing in the leads and customers you are paying for.

Where to Go from Here

I want to finish this chapter by giving you a little cheat sheet to follow, so you know which video option to target based on your needs. Here we go.

I need traffic: Run video ads; it will take you several months (if not longer) to start generating traffic from YouTube.

I need to build an audience: Build your YouTube channel, while simultaneously posting videos to your own site, too (it's okay to post the same video to your site that you've posted to YouTube).

I need to make sales: Run video ads and further refine your skills by producing marketing videos that appear on the sales pages for your products. Marketing videos need to do one of three things (and sometimes can do all of them):

1. **Demonstrate.** Video is the perfect demonstration tool. If you can demonstrate your product or service, do it.
2. **Explain.** If your product or service is tech related or may be a bit confusing to people, use your marketing video to explain what it is you do in simple terms. These are called "explainer videos" and often use cartoon-like graphics to make the complex even more simple.
3. **Build credibility.** Your face on camera can go a long way in generating sales. People don't want to buy from a business; they want to buy from a person. Whenever you can inject yourself as a real person in your marketing videos, do it.

And Finally . . .

The number-one reason people fail with web video is that they never start . . . or they start and then stop.

The plain truth is, your first few attempts at making videos will be time-consuming and frustrating and the videos themselves probably won't be very good.

This frustration is completely normal and experienced by everyone. Promise.

But the people who continue on past that pain point are the ones who find success. I've seen this happen too many times for it not to be a fact. Person A makes a few videos, quits, and struggles with their business year after year. Person B makes a few videos, then a few more, and even more. A year down the road, their business has grown by impressive numbers. And a few years down the road, they laugh at their very first videos and are so grateful they didn't quit.

There are lots of Person A. There are far fewer of Person B.

So the question for you is . . . which person do you want to be, A or B?

"Oren Michels, CEO of Mashery, explains that 'people tend to interpret having the "right" to express themselves online as implying a lack of consequences when they say stupid things.' That's not the case."

Sharlyn Lauby,
president of Internal Talent Management

Crafting a Social Media Policy for Your Organization

SO FAR WE HAVE BEEN FOCUSING on how you can personally have a Zen-like experience using social media. But what happens when your employees start tweeting and creating Facebook pages? What happens if they spill company secrets? What happens if they leave—and maybe not on the best of terms? The best action is to take precautions. Having a social media policy in place is akin to setting expectations. If I could sum up this whole chapter, I'd say a social media policy is about being smart and using common sense. And some companies have just that policy! So, you have two choices here. One, you can decide that you will just trust your team to use common sense and be smart about what they put online. It is simple, and lots of companies do use that method. Two, you can create and implement a more precise policy so everyone knows what the rules are. I use words like "policy" and "rules" very loosely. I think they can often connote a very strict interpretation, but that is not what I am trying to impress here. Think of policy as "suggested guidelines" and rules as "how to play smart."

Remember, *having a social media policy in place does not mean that you get to dictate your image. But you do get to interact responsibly in the conversation that dictates your image.* And, you get to help your employees do the same. There are great benefits to today's technology and its widespread use, but there are also some risks, as dictated by Raj Malik of Network Solutions (blog.networksolutions.com/2009/sxsw-follow-up-corporate-social-media-guidelines). As Malik says, unauthorized or inappropriate commentary or posts online can:

- Get the company, and you, into legal trouble with the United States and other government agencies, other companies, customers, or the general public
- Diminish the company's brand name by creating negative publicity for the company, owners, and partners, as well as yourself or your team
- Cause damage to the company by releasing nonpublic information or proprietary information
- Cost the company the ability to get patents or undermine its competitive advantage
- Cost you your job at the company

The following are 10 steps to creating your own social media policy.

1. **Decide where you stand.** A policy is only as good as the company that implements it. Essentially, the lines are drawn, and you have to take a stand. How far is your company willing to go in the social media sphere? Will you choose to communicate only in reaction to what someone else says? Will you be proactive in engaging the community (consumers and bloggers)? Without an overall attitude about social media, it can be very hard to create a policy. This doesn't have to be a verbal stance, but it should be a part of your company's culture. For example,

Zappos, a very successful online shoe store, encourages all their employees to partake in social media. In fact, 400 out of their 700 employees are on Twitter. Their stance is that everyone jumps in—and then uses his or her own common sense. It seems to be working for them so far!

2. **Determine what constitutes social media.** A blog and LinkedIn may easily be categorized as social media, but what about online video? What about Twitter? What really constitutes social media? You must have your own (preferably written) definition. This is especially true because new websites and tools emerge all the time. My personal definition of social media is any website or medium (including video) that allows for communication in the open. Let's say that you tell your employees not to mention an upcoming merger until you are ready to announce it. However, two employees chat about it with each other via direct messaging on Twitter, and because of a glitch, the message is made public. Did they break a rule or do direct messages on social media constitute a private forum?

3. **Clarify who owns what.** Does your company have a Facebook page that is handled by the head of HR? What happens when that person leaves? Who owns that page? That content? James C. Roberts III of Global Capital Group Law offers this: "If there is an offer letter or employment contract, it would normally state who owns what (usually the company). Absent that, the law could default to ownership by the company (but depending upon the state). On the other hand, if the company has turned a blind eye to personal use during work hours then it could be attacked. And, it will depend upon the extent to which what is created is based on company property (IP)." (Note: This is not to be construed as legal advice. Please consult with your own attorney for advice specific to your company.) To keep things simple, make sure your employees know what is theirs and what belongs to the company.

4. **Keep confidential information private.** Although other company policies may address the issue of keeping proprietary and personal information confidential, it never hurts to readdress it in terms of social networking. Because of the casual nature of these sites, it is easier to give away key information without realizing it. Even private messages aren't always secure. Each site has its own fallibilities. It is best to never share any confidential or proprietary information using social media—publicly or privately.

5. **Decide who is responsible.** Although it is important that everyone understands the company's social media policy, it is also important that one person or a team of people be responsible for managing social media efforts. If a customer does make a public complaint, who will answer it? Do they need to forward that to another department? Social media management doesn't automatically fall under the job description of the web developer, PR person, or HR manager. All employees should be encouraged to interact and represent the brand, but there should be one or a few who are proactively handling queries. The best way to find a social media advocate within the company is to seek out the one person or team of people who are most passionate about communicating with customers in such a manner. They may already be doing so without your knowing it. Seek out those people, and train them well.

6. **Dictate the rules of engagement without being a dictator.** It is a fine line to walk—allowing employees the freedom to engage and protecting the company at the same time. However, it can be done. You can't stop employees from communicating using the new media, but you can set some ground rules that work for everybody's benefit.

7. **Address taboo topics.** Although your employees probably already exercise good common sense while participating online, it never hurts to clarify specifically what is off limits. Raj Malik of Network Solutions offers this partial list:

- Topics about which the company is involved in litigation or could be in the future (e.g., policy, customer disputes, etc.)
- Nonpublic information of any kind about the company, including, but not limited to, policies and strategy
- Illegal or banned substances and narcotics
- Pornography or other offensive illegal materials
- Defamatory, libelous, offensive, or demeaning material
- Private/personal matters of yourself or others
- Disparaging/threatening comments about or related to anyone
- Personal, sensitive, or confidential information of any kind

8. **Have a system for monitoring the social sphere.** A social media policy doesn't do much good if you don't actually monitor the space where the conversation is happening. There are plenty of free and paid tools to monitor the online space. There are also firms like ours that offer reputation management services.

9. **Make training easily available.** Think win-win. Nobody likes to be bossed around, especially when it comes to his or her own social networking. However, most people are very open to learning about how to better leverage social media sites to further their own careers and brands. Most people who make mistakes online just don't know any better. If you expect your employees to use the social networking tools properly, you must provide training. What they put out there isn't just a reflection of the company; it is also a reflection of them. Make it a win-win for everybody.

10. **Have a crisis plan.** Let's say you have a perfect social media policy in place. What happens if an employee breaches it? What happens if the people you laid off decide to start a Facebook hate group? Or if a disgruntled customer

creates a YouTube video (hey, it happened to United Airlines!)? The worst action is inaction. You must act immediately if a crisis occurs. Ignoring it—or, worse, trying to bury it—will only increase the backlash. Ideally, you have already been proactive in your efforts. You have a company blog, you have a Twitter account, and you have some influencers as friends who will vouch for your company. Either way, you will need to take corrective action right away. First, contact the person responsible. Apologize, clarify, and do what you need to do to rectify the mistake. Second, make a public announcement apologizing and clarifying. Also, address steps put into place that will keep such a debacle from occurring again. In social media, transparency is crucial. This is why step 1 is, well, step 1: Decide where you stand.

"You are in the findability department. The marketing department is dead."

Todd Defren,
principal for SHIFT Communications

A Final Word on Social Media
Tools for Attracting Even *More* Business

BEFORE WE FINISH UP, I want to give you a few more tools for making the most of social media marketing.

Integrating Your Social Media Efforts

One of the biggest struggles people face in marketing with social media is figuring out how it all ties together. How does social media fit in with online marketing? What does the big picture look like? You want to integrate your social media efforts not only to save time but to reach even more people than you thought possible. Let's take a look at some ways you can tie in your social media efforts.

Revolve Your Efforts Around Your Website

This is your home base—where all the action should occur. As I've mentioned, you should do everything you can to organize your social media marketing efforts around directing traffic to your website.

However, you can also use your website to let visitors know about what social media sites you're involved with, giving them the chance to keep in touch with you in other ways. Facebook, Twitter, and LinkedIn all provide badges or buttons you can place on your website, which allow visitors to connect with you on these other sites. If you have a graphic designer or are one yourself, you can create your own.

Make It Easy to Share Your Content

If you have a blog or post articles on your website, find a way to enable one-click sharing. The easier it is to share your content, the more likely it is people will share. You will reach so many more people in this manner just by leveraging your current visitors. Give your visitors an easy way for people to tell their friends. This is why I really like the functionality WordPress provides. It is a blogging platform that you can build your entire website on. If you use WordPress, you can also download the ShareThis plug-in, which allows visitors to easily share your content on their social media sites. It can be found at www .ShareThis.com.

Social bookmarking is another way to facilitate sharing. Social bookmarking, in a nutshell, allows visitors to share their bookmarks with one another. Websites dedicated to facilitating the collection and sharing of bookmarks are a great way to attract new visitors to your website. Although there are many such sites out there, here I will focus on the three that I believe have the most potential to drive traffic to your website.

- **StumbleUpon:** StumbleUpon (www.StumbleUpon.com) is a great tool for driving long-term traffic to your website. It is my favorite social bookmarking site, because it drives quality traffic and it helps you discover quality websites. It also tends to bring a good mix of visitors.
- **Digg:** Digg (Digg.com) is a rather famous social bookmarking website, but the traffic you get from it tends to be

short-lived. Think sharp spikes of quick traffic. The audience on Digg is also partial to technology pieces.

- **Delicious:** Delicious (Delicious.com) is simple to use and has a broad audience. If you aren't familiar with social bookmarking sites and need a simple way to get started, this is a great site to get started with.

Synchronize Your Status Updates with HootSuite

Status updates, across all social media sites, are crucial to presenting and sculpting your brand. However, updating all of them can be time-consuming. The best tool I have found so far for updating all your status updates at once is HootSuite.

Initially, you have to input your login information from each of your social media sites. This takes a few minutes. HootSuite then saves all the login information, and the next time you have an important message to send out, you can do so with just one click. You log in and post a single update in HootSuite. Then, that update is automatically sent across the board to all the sites you gave HootSuite the login information for.

There may also be search engine–related benefits to setting up HootSuite that have yet to be fully unearthed. Ruth Perryman of the QB Specialists (www.TheQBSpecialists.com) sent me an email describing the way her business's Google rank shot up after she signed up for a similar site. I was definitely intrigued, so I interviewed Ruth.

How did you use a social media management platform to get ranked in Google for your search term?

Nobody really knows what Google uses to rank pages, and, worse, it's thought that their algorithm changes often. But my key search term "QuickBooks enterprise" shot from higher than 20 pages (I gave up looking after that) to page three within about a week of me signing up for the social media management platform and joining all the network sites they link to. I believe the links to my website from those social networking sites is the reason for the huge increase, because I didn't make any other changes during that period. We're also on the first page of Yahoo!, and on the fifth page of MSN/Live now, but I can't honestly say I knew what the ranking was before because I never checked. But I believe it's very likely they were also 20 or more pages in. We're tinkering with the website more now to see if we can replicate it. For instance, my staff is also signing up for this social media management platform. If we continue to climb up the page ranks, it'll be almost certain that this is the cause.

What is your social media management platform strategy?
One of my friends told me about the platform a few weeks back, and it sounded like a great way to manage Twitter-type messages and status updates. But I'm the anal sort (good to be when you're an accountant), so one rainy Sunday I went in and added all their networking sites that I didn't belong to. I posted my picture, added my website, and entered little bios. It never entered my mind that it might increase my ranking. But for the last six months, I've been just checking Google to see if I was in the top 20 yet, only to be denied week after week, and then, lo and behold, less than a week after I joined all those networking sites, I was suddenly on the third page. You could've knocked me over with a feather! In fact, when I saw I was also on the third page for Yahoo!, I couldn't help but yell—wait for it—"Yahoo!" Great name, by the way; very appropriate.

If you could share one tip or strategy with others looking to do the same, what would it be?
Carve out a day—a cold, rainy day over a weekend is perfect; after all, what else are you going to do?—and just start at the top of the platform's list of networking sites. Join them, and complete your profiles. At the very least, put in your business name and website. It's actually a nifty little tool—you enter one 140-character post, and it'll send your post to all the

microblogging and status update sites automatically (you can change your defaults so it only goes to the ones you choose). That's actually what I originally meant to use it for; the surge in page ranking was an unexpected yet delightful surprise.

Given that my company, The Marketing Zen Group, already ranks high for many of our top keywords, I have not yet tested this strategy. However, just claiming your personal name and your business name on various social media sites is a good strategy in itself. And if it does result in extra benefits, as in Ruth's case, even better!

The easiest part of social media measurement is simply counting the numbers. Website visitors, blog links, Twitter mentions, and Facebook fans are all numbers worth measuring.

Unfortunately, the numbers only tell us half of the story. Next you need to measure the sentiment of each of these social media channels. What percentage is positive versus negative? Are your efforts pushing that sentiment needle in a positive direction?

Lastly, you need to connect this all to your bottom line. You know you increased the number of mentions on Twitter, and you know that the majority of tweets were positive, but do you know how many new sales were generated as a result?

Understand this trifecta of social media measurement and you'll see success.

Andy Beal,
founder of Trackur (www.Trackur.com) and coauthor of Radically Transparent

How to Measure Your Efforts

Social media metrics is the technical term for measuring your social media marketing efforts. And, yes, this could also be a book in itself. Albert Einstein once said, "Everything that can be counted does not necessarily count; everything that counts cannot necessarily be counted." So much of social media is about building relationships and leveraging word of mouth. How do you measure goodwill? Sometimes a consumer has to hear about you 10 times before he or she will buy. You engage consumers using multiple channels, so how you do know which straw broke the camel's back?

There are some things you can measure—and you should! Here are some straightforward metrics that you can use to start measuring right away:

- **Your bottom line:** I am always surprised by how many people don't at least measure their bottom line. By "bottom line," I mean how much money you're making. How much revenue is coming in compared to how much was coming in before you started using social media?

  Social media marketing is complex, and it is sometimes almost impossible to track exactly how and why someone came to buy from you. This is because, if done correctly, social media marketing is like filling a piggy bank, each coin bringing you a bit closer to your goal. Eventually, one last coin will fill the jar; however, each coin got you a little bit closer.

  When we ask how new clients heard of us, we often get answers like, "I saw you speak once and subscribed to your newsletter. Then I friended you on Facebook. However, I had to unsubscribe for a while, because I was busy with other things. Then I saw a status update you made on Facebook to a post you wrote, and it was exactly the help I needed." Do you get the picture? Many coins, one piggy bank. Measure your bottom line!

- **Number of leads:** This is another very straightforward

metric. How many leads did you get before you implemented social media marketing, and how many leads have you gotten afterward?

- **Website visits:** Currently, Twitter is responsible for 20 percent of our company's website traffic. We use Google Analytics (a free tool provided by Google) to measure how many people visited our website and where they came from.
- **Sales cycle:** Measure how long it takes to make a sale to a new client. If your best friend was selling you a car that you needed, how long would you hesitate before buying? Given that you had the money and trusted your friend, not long! Compare that to buying a car from a dealer. How many dealers would you visit? How much research would you do? Social media marketing allows you to be that friend—the person or company that people trust.

  For instance, when prospective clients come to our company, they are often already ready to buy. And these aren't small purchases. They just have a few questions. We don't submit long drawn-out proposals or go back and forth proving that we can do the job. They already know we can, because they have seen us online. They have visited our website, read our articles, seen us on Twitter, and perhaps even seen some of my videos on ShamaTV. If you can establish your expertise online, you will find that people are more than eager to do business with you.

- **Conversion rate:** Let's say that before doing any social media marketing, one out of ten people who came to your website bought something. After you follow all the directions in this book, two out of ten people are buying. Your conversion rate just went up! Why might this be? People are more comfortable buying from brands they trust. Although you may not be Coca-Cola, you can certainly establish trust through open communication and transparency. I am more willing to buy from someone I know I can get in touch with easily than from a no-name company online. What about you?

For Executives Only! Seventeen Best Practices for Adopting Digital Marketing

Many executives between the ages of 45 and 65 are digital aliens. They were not brought up in the digital age and feel overwhelmed and sometimes fearful of the new technologies. Many struggle with the changes necessitated by engaging in digital marketing. The result is a new digital divide between companies that are fully immersed in digital applications and others that are still trying to decide if Facebook is even a good investment!

The following is a road map of 17 practices that, for the latter companies, will facilitate the adoption and successful implementation of a digital marketing program.

1. **Assess current market practices.** Determine the gaps and opportunities to position your organization in the digital world.
2. **Adopt a digital mind-set.** Gain executive understanding and buy in to the changes required to adopt a digital marketing program.
3. **Dedicate resources.** Commit staff, provide training, and allocate budget.
4. **Strategize.** Design a digital marketing strategy that incorporates your assessment, clarifies goals and brand, integrates all media, and tracks and evaluates. More than 60 percent of social media programs fail because they don't have a blueprint.
5. **Build on what you do best.** Incorporate digital media to leverage and augment successful marketing efforts already in progress.
6. **Listen, research, refine.** Monitor digital buzz and real-time customer feedback via forums, tweets, surveys, online reviews; refine your product.
7. **Give value.** Focus on giving value before expecting anything in return.
8. **Be consistent, not overpowering.** Maintain your brand; increase your digital presence through regular conversations, but don't push, overexpose, or irritate.
9. **Develop sustainable relationships.** Create conversations and take the time to interact; this is a social environment. Conversations build relationships and encourage participation. Touch your current and potential customers with regular alerts on new services, advice, and deals.
10. **Provide social sharing.** Include easy-to-access social amplification tools (social sharing buttons for Facebook, Twitter, Digg, StumbleUpon, and email) to spread the message.

11. **Cultivate satisified, loyal customers.** Focus on caring for, thanking, satisfying, and providing value for your customers. This will engender trust and encourage your customers to do your marketing for you by sharing your product with their networks.

12. **Leverage social communities.** Access related social communities that have a potential interest in or would benefit from your product. These groups can boost exposure and penetration with little additional expense.

13. **Develop an online environment as your hub.** Drive traffic to an integrated online environment, including a website, Facebook site, landing pages, and a blog.

14. **Integrate media.** Augment your traditional advertising (TV, radio, outdoor, direct mail, print) and PR with social media, mobile, and online efforts.

15. **Monitor and measure.** Track your company's digital footprint (the size and composition of your online presence), company chatter, and social mentions.

16. **Evaluate your Social Return on Investment (SROI).** Evaluate SROI as a tool for measuring a much broader concept of value. SROI incorporates social, environmental, and economic costs and benefits into decision making and helps you readjust your strategy and tactics to meet your goals.

17. **Keep current and generate a competitive edge.** Keep your "fingers on the pulse" of your business ecosystem and the changing digital environment. This responsiveness will drive innovation and competitive positioning.

Dr. Ira Kaufman,
Entwineinc.com

Wrap-Up

To wrap up, I want to leave you with three main points to take away:

1. **Strategize first.** Before you create a single profile or partake in a single online conversation, map out your overall online strategy. What will you use to attract? What will you use to convert? What will you use to transform? The tools you use to do these things will be your tactics.

2. **Be human**. Remember that behind every Twitter name or Facebook profile is a real live human being. The ultimate goal is always to connect with that person. Even if you're talking to a group, that group comprises individuals who crave personal connection and attention.
3. **Have patience**. Measure your social media efforts, but also have patience. Social media marketing is a long-term strategy; pay attention to the results you're getting as you go, but always keep your eye on the horizon.

By now, I hope you have a much better grasp of social media marketing and what it entails. I further hope you have realized that leveraging social media isn't hard; you just have to know how to use it, and it can be an incredibly powerful tool. It is truly the Zen way of achieving success!

> "Sometimes the questions are complicated and the answers are simple."
>
> Dr. Seuss

Burning Questions and Answers

Taking Questions and Dishing Out Answers and Advice

WHEN I WROTE THIS, I wanted to make sure I covered the topic of social media marketing in the most comprehensive and useful manner I could. To that end, I asked my blog readers to ask me their most pressing questions. Although most of their questions have already been covered in a general way in the previous chapters, I wanted to include some direct, specific answers as well. Because these questions come up often, I hope the answers will benefit you, too!

Q1: *Within the last decade, we've seen many technology trends come and go. In your opinion, why will social media marketing stand the test of time, outside of its being an exciting, dynamic, and ever-evolving way to market?*

A1: I don't know what social media will look like in another hundred years. I can say with much confidence that it will be here for many years to come. It may take on a different form, but its essence will not change. By "essence," I mean that people now know what it is like to have their own microphone—to have their opinions heard. You can't change that. You can't push and bully people anymore. People *will* talk, and today their messages can reach thousands. You want to leverage this power for the better, and that isn't going away anytime soon!

Q2: *Is social media marketing meant for all audiences? Is there a group for which it isn't a good fit?*

A2: The chances that your buyers aren't online are slim. Even if you serve geriatric patients, I can bet their caregivers still look for information on the internet. *How* they use social media can differ greatly. Do they just read articles but not interact? Or do they like having their own say? The sites they use can also vary. For this, you will have to research your audience. Two books I *highly* recommend reading on this subject are *Meatball Sundae* by Seth Godin and *Groundswell* by Charlene Li and Josh Bernoff. If you are marketing to baby boomers, *Dot Boom* by David Weigelt and Jonathan Boehman is also a fantastic read.

Q3: *Is it better to focus on traditional or social media?*

A3: It depends because the meaning of "traditional media" is changing. For example, it is quite common now for newspapers to have an online edition. Some are even focusing more on their online versions, and still others provide only online versions. I recently heard that email marketing is now considered traditional. Traditional marketing itself is evolving to encompass more and more. In the end, your focus should be on whatever medium allows you to reach your audience.

Q4: *How do I find truly qualified prospects online? I seem always to run around with circles of friends or peers. I find my colleagues more than prospects.*

A4: This is not an uncommon situation. It is easy to end up in the same circles, especially when your colleagues (and competitors) are also early adopters and use social media. The best way to expand your circle is to use Facebook groups to meet new people. You can even create your own Facebook group. If you use Twitter, you can search for people with similar interests or problems (that you can solve!). This is also why it is important to drive people to your website and collect their information there. They may not belong to your circle, but they may run into your website. Find a way to stay in touch with them.

Q5: *I get so many invites for Facebook applications! It spins my head. Do I say yes to all?*

A5: On the contrary, feel free to say no—liberally! Only say yes to applications and groups that resonate with your professional mission. Many applications force you to select at least seven friends to use the application yourself; it's one of the reasons you get so many application invites. Just say no! If you choose to just stick to the Facebook basics outlined in Chapter 4, you will be doing more than fine!

Q6: *If you have a new follower on Twitter, is it okay to invite him or her to join you on other networks? What is the proper etiquette here?*

A6: Yes, it is okay to invite people to join your other networks. *But* you shouldn't bombard them with requests or let this be your only communication with them. It's a good idea to get to know them first. Ask them what they do, and share information about yourself; build at *least* an acquaintance relationship. Otherwise, it looks like you are just trying to rack up your numbers, and no one likes being just a number.

Q7: *How do I find the time to interact with social media to really connect with people without spending all my time doing it?*

A7: First, find two social media networks to focus on. Then, come up with an online networking strategy that works for you. This doesn't have to be complex; it can consist of simple tasks. Let's look at a *simple* Facebook networking strategy: log on, update your status, wish your friends a happy birthday, respond to your messages, pick one person from your network to get to know better, and set up a call with him or her for the week. Fairly simple, right? It can be easy to lose track of time on social media sites, so you can even try setting up a timer. Once your thirty minutes are up, you are done! This does require some discipline on your part.

Q8: *What should you do if someone wants to be your friend on Facebook, but he does not tell you how he knows you or why he wants to be your friend? Is there a downside to accepting him as your friend if you don't know him?*

A8: This depends on your friending policy. I know some people who will only befriend those they know offline. Others will befriend anyone and everyone. You have to find the strategy that works for you. If you are planning to use Facebook as a way to meet new people, then you may want to consider accepting friendship requests from strangers. In my case, I reach more people through my blog and work than I meet personally. I have a wide audience, so I choose to connect with people via my fan page at www.Facebook.com/Shama HyderProfile. This allows me to balance privacy and accessibility. I reserve my Facebook profile only for friends I know offline.

Q9: *Does social media marketing work well for multilevel marketing businesses? I feel like my industry isn't trusted.*

A9: My experience is that social media marketing works for any type of business, but you have to figure out a way to add value to your network. Multilevel marketing schemes are an extremely misunderstood business model because of companies that ruined the industry's reputation. Social media is a great way to educate people, and you can use that to improve the way people think about multilevel marketing. Does this take time? Yes. Does it work eventually? Absolutely.

Q10: *What do you do when someone you know through your personal life posts messages on your business social media profile that don't match up with your business life?*

A10: Great question! It depends. If the message is generic or speaks to me as an individual, I don't mind it. For example, my cousins often leave "we miss you" messages on my wall. I am okay with this. This doesn't make me less professional in other people's eyes. In fact, it humanizes me even more. On the other hand, if I receive an inappropriate message from a personal friend, I quickly delete it. If it was just a silly link, I don't say anything to her. I just delete. If I feel like she may not be up-to-date on Facebook etiquette, I delete her post and then message her privately, asking that in the future she contact me privately instead.

Q11: *Why do we use war terminology ("campaign," "tactics," "strategy," "target") to refer to social media as if the people we're reaching out to are our enemies, to be attacked, pillaged, and plundered?*

A11: Good point. I am not a fan of the violent connotations either. This started because traditional marketing's view of consumers was much harsher than today's view. In the earlier days, you had to *make* someone get your message. You had to convince and convert. Today, the best strategy is to present potential customers with value and choices. It's a game changer. Unfortunately, the vocabulary has stuck, because it's what we are familiar with. If I used "approach" instead of "strategy," it might confuse some readers. Not all, but some. My goal is to communicate to be understood. For now, that involves using familiar (albeit not the friendliest) vocabulary.

Q12: *How do marketers reach business owners who say that they have no time for social media? Or those that feel social media in general is a time vampire?*

A12: Give them a copy of this book. Better yet, tell them that people are social creatures (news flash) and that people are *already* talking about their businesses online. They can either be part of the conversation or not. This is a choice every business has to make. As a marketer, you can help them strategize, give them tools, and show them how to measure. The results should speak for themselves.

Q13: *How many social networking groups should someone be in?*

A13: Focus your strategy and networking efforts on a few sites at a time. Ideally, you should focus on two social networking sites and go deep. Understand the rules, cultivate relationships, and get comfortable using them for business. My experience is that most people who join smaller or niche social sites are already part of the bigger ones. It is rare to find someone joining a new social network as an early adopter who isn't already part of a bigger one like Facebook or LinkedIn.

Q14: *When supplying content to your social sites, should you repeat the same articles and blogs, or do rewrites with completely fresh material?*

A14: Share what you currently have. There is no penalty in repeating information; you don't need fresh content for each social networking site. This is a great way to propagate your information. That being said, I don't recommend repeating yourself too much. You want to share your information without seeming like an automated machine. You want to focus on sharing the same information across several media channels, not repeating the same message on one like a robot.

Q15: *How do you know which social media site gives the best ROI for your time and effort? Do I join each new one that pops up, or do I lurk, listen, and take my time?*

A15: Lurk, listen, and take your time. Don't join every network that comes your way. My recommendations are Facebook, Twitter, LinkedIn, and now Google+ as well. You can also search for specialized social networking sites that your specific audience uses.

Q16: *Any specific marketing tips for the current tough economic times?*

A16: As someone who bootstrapped my company to success, my recommendation will always be the same. Focus on marketing techniques that provide a high return on investment—like online marketing, which costs little and does a lot. Let your current clients and well-wishers be your advertising team. Encourage and reward them for sharing with their friends. Most importantly, stay optimistic. The economic tide is always changing, but people will also always have needs and wants. The only difference in a downturn is that they get extra picky. You have to educate and encourage more than you push. My employees and clients always tease me that my favorite word to use is "leverage." But it is exactly what you have to do in this economy to succeed—and what social media allows you to do with so much ease. Leverage your past success, leverage your well-wishers, and leverage your colleagues by partnering with them. Leverage social media overall to amplify your message and credibility.

Social Media Marketing Case Studies
Highlighting Real-World Best Practices

SOCIAL MEDIA PROFILE 1:
Yvonne DiVita, Lip-Sticking
(www.LipSticking.com)

In what ways have you utilized social media sites? If you feel blogging is the cornerstone of these efforts, do you think someone can utilize these sites without having a blog?

My foray into social media was via my blog on marketing to women. It opened the door to new and exciting relationships. I met business professionals from all over the world and even from my own backyard. I was able (and still am able) to promote myself, and my business, by sharing expertise and insight, instead of selling. After the popularity of the blog brought me speaking engagements and even client referrals, I branched out into Facebook and Twitter and some other social networking sites that I have been invited to join, such as SWOM (Society for Word of Mouth) and TwitterMoms, as well as Savvy Auntie. I find them useful in building and maintaining great relationships. And I'm able to help other women learn how to market themselves on the web. This brings me recognition as an expert in my field.

I recommend a blog. Can you make a go of it without a blog? I don't think so. A blog is the sincere, personal side of yourself and your business. The blog gives the writer an outstanding opportunity to communicate value and advice without being preachy or sales-y. On the blog, it's possible to engage numerous people in many different conversations, thereby growing your reach and connection throughout the nation and the world. With other networking sites and Twitter, you can initiate the conversation and even share select parts of it. But it all goes back to the blog, where the real opportunity to be yourself exists. Business blogging is extremely helpful for new businesses, as long as the writer remembers to focus on the business and not on too much family stuff. Be professional. If you want to have a blog for family newsletter content, start a family blog.

Which has been your favorite social media site so far and why?

I'm still a blogger at heart. I *love* Twitter. It really has extended my reach and introduced me to hundreds of new people who I can tap into if I need an answer to a simple business question or if I need content to substantiate something I am writing about in my blog. But in the end, I prefer blogs to anything else.

Do you have a social media marketing strategy?

Absolutely! If you're in business, you should never engage in social media without a strategy! Mine is to give thoughtful content and advice, and receive some in return. It's a people-policy kind of strategy—I am here to support people in their business endeavors. It's not about the tools ever! It's about the people. Anything I can do to be more personal and focused on results for others makes my work worthwhile and successful.

If you could share one tip or strategy with others looking to do the same, what would it be?

My tip would be to always remember your beginnings. In the beginning of our business ventures, we are all eager to talk to experts and take in their advice. Those experts who give freely (always maintaining a level of free advice but gently letting others know that beyond that line is paid consulting) get the best results. Be selective of those you might become a mentor to—it's a wonderful way to give back, but depending on whom you choose to mentor, the time involvement could get away from you.

I'd like to remind everyone that social media is just that: a type of connection that's social. Be sociable. Be approachable. Learn good time-management skills, and understand that no one expects the world from you. Just be the person you wished someone had been for you back when you were getting started. Do this online, via social media tools and networks, and do it offline in a true face-to-face manner. Building your business by learning how to utilize social media and how to bring it offline in a face-to-face group gathering will bring you the success you endeavor to achieve. I recently wrote a blog post that quoted Shirley Chisholm, the first African American woman elected to Congress (quoting [tennis star] Arthur Ashe): "From what we get, we can make a living. What we give, however, makes a life."

SOCIAL MEDIA PROFILE 2:
Pattie Simone, CEO of WomenCentric.net
(WomenCentric.net)

In what ways have you utilized social media marketing for your business or organization?

We use social media to share our latest blog posts, site news, and member updates, to greet/connect/interact with our members and fans. We also use social media to broaden our reach, and network by tweeting interesting/relevant articles for our members, fans/followers, and potential members/fans/followers. Topics include items of interest pertaining to women small-business owners, entrepreneurs, and thought leaders, social media tips, travel deals, food stories, shopping deals, etc. Basically, we broadcast, inform, interact, and promote topics, events, news, and self-produced original and outside videos relevant to our members, potential members, fans, followers, and clients.

Which has been your favorite social media site so far and why?

Twitter is our favorite social media site. We have made so many great connections and continue to meet exciting and interesting new people every day. Many of our new members have found out about us through our efforts on Twitter. The simplicity of Twitter plus the potential to reach global prospects quickly and easily really appeals to us. Twitter's reach also makes it easier to connect with a larger audience (versus what's on Facebook or LinkedIn).

Do you have a social media marketing strategy in place?

Yes: be active and engage with our Twitter, Facebook, Google+, and LinkedIn networks. Post interesting, relevant, informative pieces or discussions. Interact as close to real time as possible. Being upbeat, helpful, and engaging with our networks is definitely the most important thing—we want to be a resource for both women professionals and those searching for women professionals.

If you could share one tip or strategy with others looking to do the same, what would it be?

Use tracking analytics sites to see how your social media strategies are measuring up. We highly recommend using the bit.ly URL shortener. The data it provides is extremely valuable.

How do you measure social media ROI?

We measure our success by the strategic expansion of our core network, new member listings, media attention, and number of RTs. All our efforts support what we are doing in other channels—networking, speaking, filming, cold calling, radio, PR, etc.

SOCIAL MEDIA PROFILE 3:
Barbara Safani, Career Solvers
(CareerSolvers.com)

In what ways have you utilized social media sites?

I used Facebook to reach out to my high school classmates. The idea caught on, and other members of the school started reaching out to classmates as well. The group currently boasts several hundred members. One former classmate reached out to me to create her bio for a new website she was launching, and another contacted me to write her résumé. Both projects resulted in endorsements on LinkedIn and MerchantCircle and additional referrals. I have used Twitter to connect with the media, and as a result, I have been quoted in a syndicated column. I am also using Twitter to drive readers to my blog and my website. On LinkedIn, I have used the Answers feature to position myself as an expert and to ask recruiters specific questions that job seekers want to know the answers to. I used their responses as the basis for several blog posts. I also use LinkedIn for clients who ask for references. This has speeded up the sales process significantly.

Which has been your favorite social media site so far and why?

Facebook. It feels like you are sitting around the living room chatting it up with your friends, colleagues, and clients. It feels like the most natural medium to me and the platform that is the most fun.

Do you have a social media marketing strategy?

I use LinkedIn to establish industry relevance, promote my brand, and position myself as an expert in my field. I use Facebook to share career information and post events. I use Twitter to share important tips and links to articles and posts with my audience. I also use it to follow my competitors and thought leaders in the careers and social media space.

If you could share one tip or strategy with others looking to do the same, what would it be?

Understand that being on a social media platform requires a certain amount of transparency, and that's not a bad thing. Sometimes it makes sense to bridge the divide between your personal and professional life. When people can see another side of you, you become more real, more trustworthy, and more credible. Letting people in to your personal life (within reason) can help build your brand and help you close more sales or foster more meaningful relationships. Social media is not just a fad. Everyone should take ownership of his or her online identity, because eventually someone is going to Google you. Put your best foot forward, and manage your online presence by creating tasteful and branded profiles on the key social media sites.

SOCIAL MEDIA PROFILE 4:
Craig Drollett, Bin Ends
(www.BinEndsWine.com)

In what ways have you utilized social media sites?

We're constantly changing and upgrading what we focus on for social tools. We use Twitter for our monthly online tastings and have developed our own site, www.TwitterTaste Live.com, as direct access to our program. We are active on Facebook as well and have recently begun video postings using the alpha of 12seconds.tv; we're currently exploring additional enhancements to both sites (www.binendswine .com and www.twittertastelive.com) that will create a much more interactive experience for our users.

Which has been your favorite social media site so far and why?

We have built the foundation of our networks on Twitter because we find that we are able to reach out to more people than with any other platform. With a quick 140-character post, we are able to reach thousands of people, literally, all over the world. Twitter and www.TwitterTasteLive.com (our online wine tasting/social media monthly series) are always the top two referrers to www.BinEndsWine.com.

Do you have a social media marketing strategy?

The issue a lot of people have with web 2.0 is not with basic use and integration but with fully understanding how to use it to disseminate a specific message. You have to adopt the lifestyle, understand why the people following you are actually following you, and understand what exactly they're hoping to get from their interaction with you. If you're constantly selling or broadcasting but not listening or interacting intelligently, then you will get tuned out. Setting up the social networks and integrating them into your own network is not a hard thing to do. The vast majority of what we use is open source and simple to integrate and upgrade. We built Twitter Taste Live based off of the Ning.com social platform. However, the ongoing project took our web design team at Saltline Studio only two days to launch.

If you could share one tip or strategy with others looking to do the same, what would it be?

Be patient, and be willing to adapt to what your users want. Don't sell, sell, sell; just get your message out, and over time you will be found.

SOCIAL MEDIA PROFILE 5:
Shel Horowitz, Principled Profit
(www.PrincipledProfit.com)

In what ways have you utilized social media sites?

To do the following:

- Build my reputation
- Build my network and develop friendships with people
- Turn some of those friendships into new income streams, speaking opportunities, etc.
- Share resources I've found (so much easier to post a tweet than go through the Digg or StumbleUpon process)
- Explore resources others have found
- Find opportunities to get covered in the media, to speak, and to pitch for work
- Vastly increase the reach of my blog by feeding it into Facebook and Plaxo
- Meet others working at the intersections between social change and marketing

Which has been your favorite social media site so far and why?

Twitter! I'm a recent convert, and I'm just amazed how easy it is to connect with people, how much useful information is exchanged, how fast my network is growing, and how helpful people are. But I find as my network grows, I miss far more than I see. I typically check three or four times a day and look two or three screens back. But now, a screen fills up in three to five minutes.

Do you have a social media marketing strategy?

More overall guiding principles: to be helpful; to put up strong content; to avoid catfights; to keep a good balance of personal, business, political, and self-promotional and to not waste my time following people who get way off on this balance; to keep trivia to a minimum; and to include some reference for context when necessary.

If you could share one tip or strategy with others looking to do the same, what would it be?

Be authentic and helpful!

Tina Su, Think Simple Now

(ThinkSimpleNow.com)

In what ways have you utilized social media sites?

I've used social media sites to expose my web content to new and existing readers. Some tips I've found useful when utilizing these sites:

- **Make many mutual friends.** Especially ones who share similar interests to those expressed on your site. Get their email addresses, and communicate with them outside of social media sites.
- **Contribute something useful to the community.** And not just spamming the site with links from your domain. Share resources and content that you've found interesting, inspiring, or useful.
- **Be personable and actively participate.** Answer emails, questions, and requests.
- **Help others.** One of my favorite sayings is, "To get what you want, help others get what they want first." It's true. Genuinely and actively help other bloggers promote their stuff; when you have something great published, they'll likely want to help you, too.

I've had great results so far. I've spent zero dollars on advertising and solely promote my site, ThinkSimpleNow .com, through social media channels. Within the first three months, the site exceeded 2,000 subscribers. Within a year, the site grew to 10,000 subscribers and 300,000 monthly page views. I am also able to earn a full-time income through the website.

Which has been your favorite social media site so far and why?
In the following order:

1. **StumbleUpon:** You can quickly gain traffic from just a few people sharing a link for your site. I also love the community on SU; people are passionate about their favorite categories. You can also consistently find useful and original content.
2. **Digg:** On the rare occasion that one of my articles hits the front page, the surge in traffic is phenomenal. It's not the traffic that I seek but the exposure that leads to new potential readers that makes Digg special.
3. **Facebook:** It gives you the opportunity to connect with people on a more personal level and follow what they're up to.
4. **Twitter:** You can easily spread useful links to many people. It's a casual and low-friction way to connect with people— even internet "celebrities."

Do you have a social media marketing strategy?

Meet and connect with as many bloggers and social media enthusiasts as possible.

If you could share one tip or strategy with others looking to do the same, what would it be?

Produce interesting, value-packed, and easy-to-understand content or services. Make it worth someone's time and attention. All these social media strategies can get you some traffic temporarily, but if you don't have the content or product to capture their attention, it's a waste of your efforts.

SOCIAL MEDIA PROFILE 7:
Adam Sell, Nine Technology

In what ways have you utilized social media marketing for your business or organization?

Since our inception, Nine Technology has led a social-only strategy for lead generation. As a startup, we felt that we needed to generate buzz with these channels and try to build our partner base before spending massive amounts of cash on traditional marketing and outreach programs. We've found a great deal of success in connecting with prospects, leads, and partners on Twitter and LinkedIn, and we've amassed nearly 200 partners through this word-of-mouth and virtual word-of-mouth system.

Which has been your favorite social media site so far and why?

I personally like Twitter most of all, because it lets you get a quick thought out into the conversation. I'm a writer, and sometimes the 140-character limit can be frustrating, but it forces me to summarize my thoughts into a short sentence and invite the conversation to continue that way. My boss, however, prefers LinkedIn, because of its workplace-based focus.

Do you have a social media marketing strategy in place?

Everybody in the company has a Twitter account, and we've encouraged all employees to tweet actively from them. It took a couple of come-to-Jesus meetings to convince some of the stalwarts in the company, but we've been successful at coordinating a concerted outreach when major news is announced. I try to maintain a three-blogs-a-week policy, as that gives us plenty of content to push out the door and bring people in with.

If you could share one tip or strategy with others looking to do the same, what would it be?

Social media is neither proactive nor reactive—it's both, depending on the circumstances. Everybody will tell you "content is king," and to some degree, they're right. Without constantly churning out new things to talk about, you'll find the conversation quickly evaporating. But listening to what people say about you is of much greater consequence. Good news takes a week to travel the world. Bad news takes an hour. You need to be listening to who's saying you're doing your job right, and you need to be listening to who's saying you're doing your job wrong. They may both have valid points, and it's up to you to figure out why one's happy and the other isn't.

How do you measure social media ROI?

On a practical level, we were Hubspot clients for a long period of time, and their tools enabled us to see actual numbers on how we were doing with SEO and social media efforts. On a more observational level, though, I've found that looking at where your leads come from is indicative of how you're doing. Over time, you can watch (through Google Analytics or other such tools) where your prospects come from and where your geographic reach grows. Before this month, we hadn't had any leads from, for example, Sweden. Geographic growth is a great indicator of your message escaping beyond the website.

Chris Geier, K2

(www.K2.com)

In what ways have you utilized social media sites?

We started our entry into social media with a basic "forums and blogs" site. We had to start somewhere, and this seemed a logical step. The goal was to simply give people a place to go and ask questions, and hopefully get answers. Our hope was that we could take this simple act of socializing a problem and grow it into a vibrant interactive community utilizing a broader effort through various forms.

Once we filled a solid need with the community site, we wanted to plan out our next step. Our next effort was to establish a presence in what we saw were the three pillars of social media. Based on additional research, we also found this to be where a fair number of our "community" spent time as well.

1. LinkedIn
2. Facebook
3. Twitter

LinkedIn has a good network of people as well as active groups and discussions. We utilize LinkedIn as a way to engage in the conversation occurring about our field of expertise (Workflow and BPM). We also maintain a corporate profile to better allow people to find us and get basic information on who we are no matter where they look (e.g., Facebook, LinkedIn, Twitter, Google, etc.).

Facebook we are still experimenting with, working to figure out what works best. We initially saw a good deal of interaction and traffic on Facebook when we started engaging there. We have pages and groups created for two of our three products and use them to post basic information and news. We also use them to share event information and let people know what we are up to and how to get involved with us in some way.

Twitter has been the most versatile tool for us. We have used it extensively. Several of us have joined up and regularly interact with the community. I personally also am constantly searching out people who have questions about K2 and/or questions about related topics such as SharePoint, Workflow, BPM, and so on. If I see people asking questions about one of our products or struggling, I try to help, and I also let them know we are here if they have feedback and/or any issues. The main goal here is just to give people another avenue to interact with us. It is very important to us that we ensure if someone has a question or has feedback that he or she has a channel to voice that, regardless of time, place, format, or medium.

Which has been your favorite social media site so far and why?

My favorite social media site thus far has been Twitter. I have found it to be the most versatile and interactive. I am regularly able to interact with K2 customers and partners. We have also been very successful in expanding our community in other ways. We are regularly able to not only get feedback from our community, but also keep them informed and help link/network them together. This helps to grow our community and make it more interactive.

Do you have a social media marketing strategy?

We have a few guiding principles in social media.

1. **Open as many channels to our community as possible.** This will enable as many people in our community to interact with us in a way that is most comfortable and easy for them.

2. **Be part of the conversation.** We need to get out there and join into the discussions that are going on about not only our product but also our industry and related genres. Doing so not only helps make people aware of us, but also allows us to expand our community and help raise the interaction levels.
3. **Make all conversations open and bidirectional.** Truly look for the interaction and not just take opportunities to broadcast.
4. **Be authentic.** Do not try to hide negative information, but rather let people see it, and then let them see how you fix it.
5. **Manage the intent.** Our intent in social media is to interact and be there for people. Ensure that all decisions made map to that.

If you could share one tip or strategy with others looking to do the same, what would it be?

The primary component of any social media effort surrounds intent and authenticity. To be truly successful, a company must take a step back and understand why they are engaging in a social media effort and then must authentically follow that intent. Not being true in this effort will eventually be seen as fraudulent and greatly damage your reputation and hinder your ability to openly interact with those you seek out. I believe that to be most effective in this genre, you must be in it for the right reasons. You must be in it for the customer and to help him or her in some way. The relationship that exists between a person or entity and others in the social network must be bidirectional; both parties must benefit for it to be effective. I see too many companies out there looking to broadcast and just push information out rather than looking to truly interact and listen. They often say they are there to listen, but their true intent is often unveiled at some point.

I highly recommend before anyone ventures out there and starts talking to people through social media that he or she listen first. Get a better understanding for who people are, where they are, and what they are saying. Then seek to be part of the conversation.

Heather Whaling, Costa DeVault

(CostaDeVault.com)

In what ways have you utilized social media sites?

In December 2008, Costa DeVault partnered with the Coalition for the Homeless of Central Florida to add social media to its already strong public relations and marketing efforts. Costa DeVault assisted with initial research, listening, and strategy development. The Coalition focused on five primary goals:

1. Increase online brand recognition.
2. Reach a new demographic.
3. Increase communication, and create a dialogue with donors, volunteers, advocates, and stakeholders.
4. Position the Coalition as an authority on homelessness.
5. Encourage active involvement with the Coalition.

Per the recommendations in the plan, the Coalition created a blog, as well as Facebook and Twitter accounts. (They also established YouTube and Flickr accounts, which are in use but are not as active.) Next, the organization identified a staff person who would be responsible for monitoring and participating in social networks—in addition to her existing PR and marketing responsibilities. Specifically, her mission was to participate in social networks to connect with local residents and businesses.

Which has been your favorite social media site so far and why?

The combination of Facebook, Twitter, and the blog have worked well for the Coalition. One by itself wouldn't be nearly as effective. The Coalition has been able to leverage the interplay between the three networks and the Coalition's existing website, each of which reaches a different audience, providing opportunities to repurpose content. Instead of reinventing the wheel, a blog post can be shared on Twitter and Facebook. Likewise, a Flickr album can be posted to all three networks. By understanding how the sites complement each other, the Coalition has been able to extend their social media efforts to three networks without generating three times the work.

Do you have a social media marketing strategy?

Yes! Costa DeVault and the Coalition are firm believers in taking a strategic approach to social media. After all, you need to be able to justify that time spent on Twitter or blogging is a good use of resources. For the Coalition, that meant establishing measurable objectives, such as "increase web traffic by 10 percent," "be mentioned on outside blog posts at least 12 times per year," and "obtain bulk donations of specific in-kind items at least three times a year from social media 'asks.'"

To ensure their efforts aligned with their objectives, the Coalition began the process with research. Before participating in any online conversations, the Coalition took the time to understand which networks are most used by the people they're trying to reach. In addition, the Coalition listened to conversations already taking place to familiarize themselves with each network's subculture—a key part to social media success.

After the research phase, the Coalition laid the groundwork for their own social media efforts, created employee guidelines for social media participation, created profiles on targeted sites, and began to add content and participate in discussions. Evaluation is a key component to their social media engagement. Is their network growing? Are people engaging and interacting with the content they create? Is traffic to their website increasing? Is the network strong enough to make in-kind donations?

If you could share one tip or strategy with others looking to do the same, what would it be?

Many nonprofits and businesses don't have the resources to create an entire "social media department." Instead, they need to integrate social media into their current responsibilities. A tip to make that more manageable: instead of creating a profile on every network, begin by engaging just a few. Get the hang of those, become a valued member of the network, and then think about expanding your presence. The Coalition chose Facebook, Twitter, and blogging because they align with their overall goals. Yes, you need to monitor keywords on other networks, but that doesn't mean you need to maintain an active presence everywhere. For most organizations, that's just not realistic.

The Coalition can provide a litany of statistics to illustrate the value of their social media efforts—including Twitter followers; Facebook fans; blog traffic, which continues to increase every month; and inbound links. But the most effective way to demonstrate the value of social media isn't in these metrics. Social media matters to the Coalition because when they needed extra help, their online network—people who were strangers just months ago—stepped up to the plate.

The economic turbulence led to a drastic drop in food donations from individuals and in the food supplies available from local food banks. To help meet the shortage facing the Coalition, they decided to test the strength of their online network by launching a bold challenge to the local community: the "Orlando 'Can' Care Challenge." This social-media-driven food drive was promoted via Twitter, Facebook, and the organization's blog.

During the weeklong challenge, the Coalition tweeted and Facebooked updates as new donations were brought in and posted photos to Flickr of each donation or group. By the end of the week, with only a few hours of staff time invested in the project, the Coalition was surprised to learn that their network produced 1,000 pounds of food.

That's just one example that illustrates why the time spent building and cultivating an online network is time well spent for the Coalition for the Homeless.

In what ways have you utilized social media sites?

We used the social media websites to find and get in touch with the proper people who could become sympathetic to our cause and help us bring awareness about the discrimination and persecution of the Greek-Catholic minority in Romania.

Our activity is a little bit different from that of most of the nonprofit organizations in the United States; therefore I would like to briefly describe what we do so that you can better understand why and how we used the social media websites.

The Romanian Greek-Catholic Association, of which I am president, supports the Greek-Catholic minority in Romania, which is currently facing a cultural and religious cleansing. In 1948 the communist regime abolished the Greek-Catholic Church in Romania and persecuted its bishops, priests, and believers for their religious views. After the fall of communism in Romania in 1989, despite the fact that our Church was recognized again by the government, the discrimination and persecution continued, hundreds of thousands of Greek-Catholic believers continuing to have their rights violated. Along with the pressure on our people, the Romanian government started a national campaign to destroy the Greek-Catholic heritage, with tens of our churches being demolished or destroyed in the last two decades. The U.S. Department of State reported these violations and abuses against our community in many reports during the years.

The main challenge that we had was the fact that most Americans didn't know anything about these abuses taking place in Romania; therefore, the first thing that we did was build a website to expose this situation. The website was optimized for search engines, and we used many of the techniques related to search engine marketing in order to get more exposure to our website and have it well ranked for certain keywords that were related to our cause.

Our first approach after the launch of the website was to use the regular media to expose the situation in Romania. We sent a press release out using one of the media wire websites. We also sent the press release directly to the main newspapers in the United States, but the exposure was very limited.

Considering the amount that we paid to distribute the press release versus the return in coverage, we soon realized that this is not the path to go if we want to help our community in Romania. We learned from experience (and out of our own pocket) that in the long term, it is better to build a relationship with somebody who writes about a subject related to our cause and make that person aware this way about the situation in Romania than to just spam him or her with press releases. This is the moment when we switched the strategy and we started using the social media websites to find and get in touch with people who could become supportive of our cause.

We started using LinkedIn, Facebook, and Twitter to find journalists, bloggers, or any other type of writers who were writing about religious affairs, foreign affairs, human rights, or any other domain that was connected somehow to our cause.

Using this approach, we were able to find and get in touch with a lot of writers; many of them asked for more details about the situation in Romania, and some of them even wrote a piece or republished our press releases. This was a great chance for me to establish a personal relationship with many of them. We had many of them assisting us with advice or even helping us write press releases. One of them recently started her own radio talk show and invited me for an interview at the end of September. Without the social media websites, I don't think we would've been able to find so many people supportive of our cause.

Which has been your favorite social media site so far and why?

In our case, the social media website that helped us the most was LinkedIn.

We were using Facebook and Twitter as well, but LinkedIn was by far the best website to find and get in touch with people who could help our cause.

We had a very specific group of people that we initially targeted, and LinkedIn offered us the best solution to find them.

I was amazed by the search options provided by LinkedIn as well as by the search results. Because there are so many search options, you can target your search very well. Also, the groups on LinkedIn offer you a very good chance to get to know experts and to follow discussions from certain fields. The Q&A option on LinkedIn offers you the chance to get advice from some of the best experts out there. I myself posted a few questions on LinkedIn, and I was amazed by how many people offered their expertise on the issue that I addressed.

If you really want to get in touch with professionals and learn from them, I would strongly recommend LinkedIn.

Do you have a social media marketing strategy?

I would rather say that I have certain rules that I follow instead of a defined social media marketing strategy. Because of the rapid changes in the technology, web applications, and new tactics that are discovered for how to use these new web applications, it is very hard to write a strategy in stone. Here are a few of the rules that I follow:

- **Objective.** Before you start planning anything, you have to decide exactly what your goal or objective that you want to achieve is.

- **Know the appropriate tactics that you can use or afford to achieve your objective.** If you have enough money, you can hire a PR firm to take care of everything for you. If you don't, then you have to identify from the tactics available out there those that you can use or afford to accomplish your objective. For example, you can send a press release to all the journalists in the United States using one of the newswire services available online, but it will cost you a few thousand dollars. This tactic might be very effective for your cause, but can you afford it?
- **Planning.** Once you've defined the clear objective and identified the tactics that you can use, you have to create a plan or a strategy for how to use these tactics to achieve your goal.
- **Execution.** Put your plan in action.
- **Stay informed.** Try to stay up-to-date with news related to social media marketing. New tactics can be developed in this field that you were not aware of when you started your campaign.
- **Be flexible.** Learn from your own mistakes, and adjust your plan. This might include adjusting the tactics that you use, either because you realized that one of them is not working or because a new one was developed, or changing your objective because you realized that it is unachievable.

If you could share one tip or strategy with others looking to do the same, what would it be?

Before you start your campaign, find out the story behind the campaigns that were successful as well as those that failed. It is better to learn from somebody else's mistake than from yours.

Social networking means interacting with people virtually. But like when you interact with people face-to-face, the other person can react in a different way from what you expected. Keep your good manners, and don't take it personally; just move forward.

Karen Maunu, Love Without Boundaries

(www.LoveWithoutBoundaries.com)

In what ways have you utilized social media sites?

We started by using a blog to tell the stories of the kids. Telling the stories of the children is so important, because it shows the true difference that is being made. In December 2008, our website was hacked into, and for a while we were without a website. We were still receiving children who needed care—some who needed emergency surgery—for whom we could no longer raise funds. Someone told us about the Facebook Giving Challenge sponsored by the Case Foundation that was through Facebook Causes. We are all moms, and none of us had a Facebook page at that time, but our kids did. We braved this brand-new world of social media to see if there would be any way we could compete in this contest. It didn't take long before we were helping to sign up all of our friends, family, and anyone else who would help. To win the contest, you had to make at least a $10 donation for your vote to be counted. There was a daily contest of the most unique donations, and each day you could win $1,000 (we won 13 times), and then over the whole contest period (50 days), the most unique voters would win $50,000—and we won! We had so many people helping—college students going up and down dorm floors, nurses who brought their computers to work, people who sat in Starbucks trying to get voters. We had a slogan: for $10 you can save 10 lives. In China, a heart surgery is $5,000, so winning $50,000 meant we could heal 10 children—and we did.

This was the start of our social media success. We are now using our Cause page to update people on the children we are helping, and we get donations almost on a daily basis. We also have over 90,000 people following us. We feel that because we were already an online virtual foundation, it really helped us to mobilize people to be able to help with getting people to help.

We post stories of the kids on our Facebook Cause page and also on our own FB pages. Our stories become viral in that once a story or a photo is posted, many other volunteers or supporters will post it on their pages, too. Social media has become larger than just one person posting; it has become a community of people spreading our stories.

The success on Facebook has helped us to launch into other sites, too. We are also using Twitter and LinkedIn. Twitter has also been very successful for us, allowing us to personally connect with people and tell our story.

Which has been your favorite social media site so far and why?

Facebook, because we are able to actively get donations from our supporters and share the stories of our kids. From this, our stories are spread all over—so many more people are learning about what LWB does by each of us posting in addition to our Cause page. It is a great place for people to stay updated on what we are doing.

Do you have a social media marketing strategy?

Love Without Boundaries has been well known in the Chinese adoption community, and our goal for social media has been to break outside of this group and to have more people know about our work. When we started branching outside the adoption world, our goal was try to get as many people as possible to learn about our work. We wanted people to see how hard we work and to learn about how this virtual worldwide foundation of over 150 volunteers from 12 countries and 36 states is able to help more than 1,500 children a year. We knew that if people could just hear about us, they would want to learn more and help. It is working! We also want to educate people on adoption and let people know how to adopt. So far, at least one family I talked to on Twitter is in the process of adopting.

Love Without Boundaries is an almost all-volunteer foundation. To keep our overhead the very lowest possible, we don't have an office. We all work out of our homes. Social media has become an extension of how we were already working—online. The Facebook staff and the Case Foundation were shocked that a small charity of moms was able to win against the "big" charities. The reason that we were able to was because we already did so much work online.

If you could share one tip or strategy with others looking to do the same, what would it be?

The one tip that we would offer is to be genuine, honest, and transparent. When people can see who you really are, they will join in and start to spread your message, too. It is like a large bandwagon that others start hopping on, and with this, your message starts spreading far and wide.

SOCIAL MEDIA PROFILE 12:

Justin Winter, Cofounder of DiamondCandles.com

(DiamondCandles.com)

In what ways have you utilized social media marketing for your business or organization?

We utilized social media (Facebook most readily) to test our innovative product idea back in February of this past year, receive feedback about our products, develop our refined product after our minimum viable product launch, create a community that encourages fans and customers to come back very regularly, and develop ongoing feedback about future scents to aid us in our new product development.

Do you have a social media marketing strategy in place?

We make earth-friendly, all-natural soy candles that each contain a ring worth either $10, $100, $1,000, or $5,000. Because people have the excitement of not knowing which type of ring is inside their candle, an extremely high percentage of our thousands of customers take pictures of their rings once they get them out of their candles and upload those pictures to our Facebook page. This encourages people to come back and see the latest posted rings and who received rings worth $100+. We commonly hear that people are becoming "addicted" to Diamond Candles and our Facebook page, coming back to our page multiple times a week to see the latest "ring reveal" pictures. We have also encouraged and successfully utilized video with YouTube where people record "ring reveal" videos of them pulling their rings out of their candles and showing them to the camera.

Which has been your favorite social media site so far and why?

We would say that Facebook has certainly been our "home base" in terms of engagement and reaching our existing fans and those friends in their networks. We have a social media marketing strategy in place that has been extremely succsessful, to the point of close to 100 user-generated videos on YouTube and over one million fans on Facebook.

If you could share one tip or strategy with others looking to do the same, what would it be?

Create value in your product or service that inspires people in some way and then figure out a way to utilize social media to bring together people who have a passion for your products and services. Simply having a good social media strategy with the latest tools will do nothing if you have bland, undistinguished products that no one cares about. Good products can't help but be successful even with a nominal social media strategy.

How do you measure social media ROI?

For ROI we frequently use Facebook to drive traffic to different pages on our site, so that we can measure traffic via Google Analytics as well as measure that traffic against sales: for example, every visitor we get directly from YouTube is worth approximately X dollars.

Discussion Questions

A Guide to Sparking Engagement on the Topic of Social Media

WHEN I WROTE the first edition of this book, I never could have guessed that in addition to being a guide for business leaders, it would also come to serve as a popular textbook on the topic of social media. Emails, tweets, and messages from professors and students around the world inspired me to add this chapter. Whether you are trying to assess your own social media strategy or using this text to teach others, I hope you will find this addition helpful.

1. Why is determining your target audience so crucial?
2. How can a website attract, convert, and transform at the same time?
3. What does it mean to use the right online "voice" for your brand?
4. How can you make a blog compelling for your audience?

5. What does the search engine optimization (SEO) process entail?
6. How do you perform keyword research?
7. What is the difference between a Facebook profile, page, and group? When is each best utilized?
8. In the age of social networks, why does a website still matter?
9. What should an ideal social media policy address?
10. Why is the audience's brand more important than the company's brand online?
11. How can an organization build around the identity of their target market?
12. How can you best engage an audience on Facebook?
13. What is your personal philosophy or friending policy on social media?
14. What are the elements of a strong LinkedIn profile?
15. How does Twitter differ from LinkedIn and Facebook?
16. What are some best practices when utilizing hashtags on Twitter?
17. How are social and search merging? (Think: +1 on Google Plus.)
18. What is a personalized search?
19. What are the elements of a strong online video?
20. What are a few things a company's internal social media policy should address?
21. What are some ways in which a company can monitor and boost their online reputation?
22. Why is listening so important on the web?
23. What are some metrics through which social media return on investment (ROI) can be measured?
24. What is the best way to handle a negative review or comment on a social network?
25. How do you think social media will evolve in the next two years? Five years?

Index

Zappos employees on, 197
Twitterfeed, 122
Twitterific, 122
Twitter Mobile, 122

U

ÜberTwitter, 122
Udemy, 189
underline tags, 46
unfollowing, on Twitter, 110–113
United Airlines, 200
URL naming, 42
URL-shortening services, 112
USB condenser mic, 177
user experience, 49
username
    Facebook, 76, 84
    Twitter, 102, 106

V

video, 173–194
    choosing options for, 192–193
    equipment for making, 174–180
    on Instagram, 141
    on Snapchat, 149, 150
    as teaching tool, 188–190
    video ads, 190–192
    on websites or blogs, 187–188
    on YouTube, 180–187
video ads, 173, 190–192
video cameras, traditional, 176
video editing software, 177–179
video lights, 179–180
Videos app (Facebook), 94
Vistage, 109
vocabulary of marketing, 215–216
von Rosen, Viveka, 134

W

websites, 17–29
architecture of, 40–42
authority of links from, 48–49
as best conversion tool, 11
blogs added to or hybrid with, 26–29
and content marketing, 25–26
elements of great websites, 21–25
EMS (Educating, Marketing, and Selling) on, 20–21
first impressions of, 19–20
mentioned in YouTube bumpers, 187
mobile-friendly, 20
quality of, 19–20
reasons for having, 18
search engine rankings of, 32 (*see also* search engine optimization [SEO])
video on, 187–188
website visits, measuring, 207
Web Video University, 173
Whaling, Heather, 237–240
Wibbels, Andy, 25
Wikipedia, 101, 127
Wildfire, 92
Winter, Justin, 248–249
WomenCentric.net, 221–222
WordPress, 26–28, 202
World Wide Web Consortium, 24

Y

YMCA (Dallas), 65
Young Entrepreneur Council, 78
YouTube, 173, 180–187
    channels on, 181
    formulas for videos, 185–187
    identifying keywords for, 183
    keywords for, 183–185
    video ads on, 190–191

Z

Zappos, 197

About the Author

Called the "Zen Master of Marketing" by *Entrepreneur* magazine and the "Millennial Master of the Universe" by *Fast Company*, Shama Hyder is a visionary strategist for the digital age.

She is the bestselling author of *The Zen of Social Media Marketing* and an acclaimed international keynote speaker who's been invited to share the stage with the world's top leaders, including President Obama and the Dalai Lama.

As the Founder and CEO, she's led the award-winning integrated online marketing and digital PR firm Marketing Zen Group to become a global industry leader. Her company has been honored by both the White House and the United Nations as one of the top 100 U.S. companies run by a young entrepreneur, as curated by Empact100.

A trusted media expert and sought-after TV personality, Shama is a frequent contributor on Fox, Bloomberg, CNBC, MSNBC, and more. As a thought leader, she's been featured in many major publications, including the *New York Times*, the *Wall Street Journal*, *Entrepreneur*, *Inc.* magazine, and *Forbes*.

Shama has been listed as a 25 Under 25 entrepreneur by *BusinessWeek* and a 30 Under 30 entrepreneur by *Inc.* magazine. She was recently named to the 2015 *Forbes*' 30 Under 30 list of movers and shakers.

For information on booking Shama for a keynote or serving as a brand ambassador, or for media queries, please visit:

www.ShamaHyder.com

"Want to build a likeable brand that attracts customers and stands out? If so, you need *Momentum*. Actionable and easy to digest, this book helps you unlock the code for marketing success in the Digital Age."

—Dave Kerpen, *New York Times* bestselling author of *The Art of People*

Marketing in today's digital age has become overwhelmingly complex—but it doesn't have to be. Success lies in stepping above of the clutter and understanding the new principles of digital marketing.

To this complicated and fast-moving world, bestselling author, renowned marketer, and award-winning entrepreneur Shama Hyder brings her uniquely Zen approach in *Momentum: How to Propel Your Marketing and Transform Your Brand in the Digital Age.*

In *Momentum*, Shama draws on her experience guiding clients ranging from small businesses to Fortune 100s to demystify the marketing landscape and provide you with the digital foresight you need to operate effectively in an increasingly digital world. Using key principles, she demonstrates how to transform your current approach into an effective, struggle-free, ROI-driven strategy.

Before you invest in another marketing strategy, take a step back. Don't waste enormous amounts of time, energy, and money on the wrong strategies and approach for your customers, industry, and market. Whether you're a young business or an established company, let *Momentum* teach you how to thrive.

shamahyder.com